T0362345

BUILDING SUSTAINABLE LEGACIES

THE NEW FRONTIER OF SOCIETAL VALUE CO-CREATION

A practitioner-oriented journal from Greenleaf Publishing, published in partnership with Business School Lausanne

WRITING FROM THE FUTURE

Breaking with academic tradition, this journal offers a unique selection of articles that are written by looking at the future challenges first and then translating these into present times. The right-aligned layout is a material way of reminding us of the fact that "no problem can be solved from the same level of consciousness that created it" (A. Einstein).

PAST   **FUTURE**

⟵――――――――――――――――――――――――――――――――――⟶

OUR FOCUS

We provide hands-on, pragmatic and user-friendly research, suggestions and case studies as a resource for organisations that are committed to implementing sustainability. It is high time to build bridges between business and academia, with the clear purpose of helping business become truly sustainable.

There are four dimensions to the journal:

1. Understand sustainability challenges
2. Specific dimensions of business sustainability
3. Exciting new solutions to implement
4. Case studies of leading business examples

In addition, we will produce a special issue annually dedicated to an important theme.

UNDERSTANDING CHALLENGES
NEW SOLUTIONS
DIFFERENT DIMENSIONS
BUSINESS EXAMPLES

FEATURING THOUGHT LEADERS OF THE FUTURE

We are featuring professionals from around the world who are at the forefront of knowledge creation: they are pursuing a part-time doctoral sustainable business degree while working actively in various industries worldwide.

Print subscriptions are available for *Building Sustainable Legacies*. The journal is free to access online and can be downloaded directly from the Greenleaf website: www.greenleaf-publishing.com/bsl

BUILDING SUSTAINABLE LEGACIES
THE NEW FRONTIER OF SOCIETAL VALUE CO-CREATION

General Editor Katrin Muff,
Business School Lausanne, Switzerland

Publisher Anna Comerford, Greenleaf Publishing, UK
Production Editor Sadie Gornall-Jones, Greenleaf Publishing, UK
Illustrator Klaus Elle **Designer** Yasmina Volet

CORRESPONDENCE

Building Sustainable Legacies encourages response from its readers to any of the issues raised in the journal. All correspondence is welcomed and should be sent to the General Editor c/o Greenleaf Publishing, Aizlewood's Mill, Nursery St, Sheffield S3 8GG, UK; journal@bsl-lausanne.ch

For more information about *Building Sustainable Legacies*, see the journal homepage at www.greenleafpublishing.com/bsl.

SUBSCRIPTION RATES

Building Sustainable Legacies publishes three times a year. The journal is free to access online and can be downloaded directly from the Greenleaf website at: www.greenleaf-publishing.com/bsl. Print subscriptions can be purchased directly from Greenleaf Publishing. Email: sales@greenleaf-publishing.com or order from our website: www.greenleaf-publishing.com/bsl.

Annual print subscription
Individuals: £80.00/€112.50/US$150.00
Organisations: £180.00/€240.00/US$320.00

Building Sustainable Legacies
Greenleaf Publishing Ltd, Aizlewood Business Centre, Aizlewood's Mill, Nursery Street, Sheffield S3 8GG, UK
Tel: +44 (0)114 282 3475 Fax: +44 (0)114 282 3476 Email: sales@greenleaf-publishing.com.

www.greenleaf-publishing.com.

ADVERTISING

Building Sustainable Legacies will accept a strictly limited amount of display advertising in future issues. It will also be possible to book inserts. Suitable material for promotion includes publications, conferences and consulting services. For details on rates and availability, please email sales@greenleaf-publishing.com.

Illustrations throughout *Building Sustainable Legacies* are supplied by and reproduced with the kind permission of Klaus Elle. Illustrations are an integral part of the journal's design and may not be representative of a contributor's article where it appears on the same page. For more information please contact General Editor Katrin Muff at katrin.muff@bsl-lausanne.ch

MIX
Paper from
responsible sources
FSC® C013604

Printed in the UK on environmentally friendly, acid-free paper from managed forests by CPI Group (UK) Ltd, Croydon

BUILDING SUSTAINABLE LEGACIES

THE NEW FRONTIER OF SOCIETAL VALUE CO-CREATION

ISSUE 5

Theme Issue: **Reframing the Game: The Transition to a New Sustainable Economy, A Special Issue of Building Sustainable Legacies**

Guest Editor:

Mike Townsend, Founder and CEO Earthshine

ISBN: 978-1-78353-511-8

print ISSN 2053-8898   *online* ISSN 2053-8901

Greenleaf PUBLISHING

About Greenleaf Publishing

Greenleaf Publishing was founded in 1992, the year of the first Rio Earth Summit, and is now the world's leading independent sustainability publisher, specializing in social responsibility, business ethics, environmental policy and management, future business strategy and practice, and sustainable development. Greenleaf has worked in partnership with some of the largest multilateral, governmental and corporate organisations involved in sustainable development, including PRME, the UN-backed Principles for Responsible Management Education; UNEP; the UN Global Compact; the WBCSD; the Dutch government; Amnesty International; the International Business Leaders Forum; and the ILO. Greenleaf has published book series on stakeholder management, business education for sustainability, system innovation for sustainability and responsible investment, as well as a number of responsible business case study series. The Greenleaf Publishing/PRME book series was launched recently.

In 2013, Greenleaf and GSE Research launched the Sustainable Organization Library (SOL), the largest specialist online library in the field of sustainability and social responsibility, consisting of 8,000 papers, chapters and case studies drawn from nearly 600 books and journal volumes. It comprises content published by Greenleaf and a number of partner organisations including EFMD (the European Foundation for Management Development), AMACOM, OXFAM International and Practical Action Publishing. See www.greenleaf-publishing.com/sol for further details.

For more information visit www.greenleaf-publishing.com.

About Business School Lausanne

Business School Lausanne (BSL) is a leading innovator in business education and ranks 3rd in Switzerland (QS 2012-13 Top 200 Global Business Schools). The school's ACBSP accredited degree programs include BBA, Masters, full-time modular MBA, Executive MBA and DBA programs. BSL also provides Executive Training in General Management, Corporate Finance (with preparation for the CFA Level I examination) and Sustainable Business (in collaboration with the University of St Gallen). BSL takes a pragmatic approach to learning by applying theory to practice and is backed by a multidisciplinary faculty of business professionals. BSL attracts students from around the world, creating a multicultural environment of more than 60 nationalities. Established in 1987, BSL is the co-founder of the 50+20 initiative on Management Education for the World (www.50plus20.org) in partnership with the Global Responsible Leadership Initiative (www.grli.org) and the Principles of Responsible Management Education (UN backed PRME).

For more information visit www.bsl-lausanne.ch.

Issue 5

Mike Townsend
Founder and CEO Earthshine

WELCOME TO THIS SPECIAL EDITION OF THE *BSL Journal*, with our focus on the transition towards a sustainable economy.

When I set out on a journey in search of Capitalism 2.0, a few years ago, I was surprised at what I found—not just in terms of the range of possibilities for a more sustainable system, nor the level of radical change that will be required to deliver a real shift in our economies and our lives. The real surprise was the extent to which many of the potential solutions are already available.

The more I looked, the more I found—and, viewing the scene through a wider lens of **sustainable economics**, it became possible to see the pieces of a very interesting jigsaw come together, bringing into focus an attractive picture of a new, vibrant, attractive, and sustainable economic operating system.

Another important insight came from reflecting on the scope of the changes needed. If we do what is truly required, if we no longer seek to exploit people and resources, in the name of accumulating and concentrating wealth—if we no longer focus on the primary interests of financial capital, can we still call it Capitalism?

If what we are left with is a new and sustainable system that no longer resembles Capitalism—what would we call it? **Sustainable Economy** just seemed like a more appropriate working title—although, I am sure the debate will rumble on.

I also found something important for the soul—genuine cause for hope, generated by the very real sense that a new system is already manifesting— *an economy within which people and businesses are able to prosper, within planetary limits*. A quiet revolution is already under way—if we could just allow it to flourish.

Hope often travels hand-in-hand with frustration. I could also see that, while a new system is desirable and possible, and that change is already under way, we are currently nowhere near a tipping point, whereby the new system takes over from the old, rendering it obsolete, and transforming into a new (sustainable) mainstream. There is still a very long way to go.

These sparks of hope and frustration led to further insights and a realisation that it might be possible to help accelerate the transition, by promoting greater awareness of the issues and the very real possibilities—ultimately, to enable more conscious choices by people, businesses, and our civic leaders, to start the migration towards a better system.

And so, the Sustainable Economy Project was born, out of a desire to create a better economic system—coupled with a passion to encourage a *progressive form of economic activism* that will help achieve this aim.[1]

Our initial agenda for change focuses on a number of key leverage points—from changing the goals and mechanics of our system of economy, to new models of business success and investing, new financial and banking systems, new institutions and greater systemic resilience, re-localised economies, to new education curricula and models for learning. There is much work to be done.

We have been quietly establishing the infrastructure to help amplify our efforts around the world, through our growing network of Sustainable Economy Hubs, ambassadors, change agents, and media partnerships—all in support of accelerating the tipping point in the transition towards a sustainable economy.

We believe that progressive business schools and universities play a major role in forming the new economy. By expanding their remit, they can act as catalysts in each region, shifting the conversation and creating a shared agenda for change within their respective business and political communities:

▶ Spreading awareness of the real possibilities for a better way—that we do not have to be constrained by the current dysfunctional paradigm

▶ Shifting the conversation in the mainstream of business, education, political and public life—building a practical bridge between these constituencies

▶ Extending the debate on key issues, like how we get capital to move from old to new economy, how we create new business models, and so on

We also have a plan, configured with an eye on the bigger picture, but also to enable manageable and practical steps towards the ultimate aim of accelerating the tipping point in system change. The next step on this life-affirming journey is what you see here today—the *Sustainable Economy Special Edition of the Building Sustainable Legacies Journal*.

Each of the contributions in this Journal helps to challenge our views on what is possible and also provides us with concrete actions on how we can make genuine progress. Many of the themes also resonate with the Sustainable Economy Project's agenda for change.

We open with Paul Polman—the pioneering business leader and CEO with Unilever. Polman sets the pace, with his inspirational views on the instrumental role of business in generating a radical shift in our economies, with 2015 seen as a pivotal year. Polman reminds us that businesses have a major impact in terms of their sustainability footprint, but they are also key players in terms of their ability to influence change at scale; by harnessing their energy, expertise and resources they can drive transformational change at a systemic level. He urges us to be "more".

---

1 For further information on the Sustainable Economy Project please visit www.the-sustainable-economy.org

That we need to be playing a different game is becoming increasingly recognised. Even mainstream commentators like the FT's Martin Woolf are calling for new and radical approaches in the running of our economies. Isabel Sebastian picks up this challenge with great gusto, and makes a great case for promoting **Wellbeing Economics** as a means of re-framing the game of economy and commerce. She includes practical proposals for the business and policy agendas—and how we can look beyond CSR to create the dynamic space for genuine business and economic transformation.

Transformation necessarily requires us to rethink our institutions, including our legal frameworks—do they adequately support our aims, or do they hinder the changes we need to make?

Business law is not usually included in the discourse on how to achieve a sustainable future and, thankfully, Beate Sjafjell helps us to redress the balance. Sjafjell recognises that neither the voluntary contribution of business, nor the current regulatory framework is sufficient in driving the level of change that is needed. She puts forward an elegant argument for reforming company law—what she refers to as the regulatory ecology of companies—leading us to solid proposals, not just for regulation, but also practical actions that companies can adopt. To encourage the shift away from business-as-usual, Sjafjell proposes that the duties of the board should encompass the drawing up of a long-term, life-cycle based business plan. Radical, practical—and, ultimately, good business sense.

Another key enabler for radical change is, of course, leadership—and transformational leadership requires the *right mindset*. Jeanrenaud and her colleagues offer us the 'One Planet' mindset, as a powerful lever for transforming self, business and society, in the contested transition towards a sustainable economy. They help us to understand what a one planet mindset is and how this state of being provides an essential condition, if we are to frame business and economics in a way that will truly enable a sustainable future. They explore five managerial mindsets that need to be integrated with sustainability thinking to provide the essential context and framing of global challenges that will enable us to rediscover *purpose* in business.

Leaders, of course, need roadmaps and models—to help them communicate the nature of their journeys, and how they will be made. Which models work best: should we create top-down mandates, or should we try to shape more organic and grassroots oriented movements for change, from the bottom-up? Which route will be more effective? Jill Bamburg helps us to see that we should waste little time on this sterile debate, and through her work on change models, facilitated by her **2x2 to change the world**, she helps us to see that it is, indeed, all good work.

In developing all the new approaches required for change—just a few of which we touch on in this Journal—we start to gain a deeper appreciation of the value and the instrumental role of education. If we don't research and teach the right things, how can we hope to gain the skills and insights that will enable us to change the world in a robust manner?

Notwithstanding the trailblazing efforts of a few leading lights, Suzanne Benn and her colleagues note that business schools are often lagging other sectors in recognising the growing importance of sustainability concerns in business decision-making. As a result, emergent themes such as cooperative capitalism or new business models are neglected in business school curricula. Through the lens of the **boundary objects** Benn and her colleagues facilitate knowledge sharing around environmental and social aspects of corporate sustainability. They propose that both educators and their students should transcend disciplinary boundaries, and engage with knowledge from different disciplinary areas, to facilitate a systematic and integrated approach to sustainability.

Going further into the mechanics of transformation, Katrin Muff introduces the **Collaboratory**—a methodology that provides an exciting template for radical re-imagination and redesign of business schools, in finding a mission that is relevant to the challenges of our time and which makes a meaningful contribution to society. Muff shares new perspectives on *finding purpose*, developed through partnership and participation. Her approach is engaging and deep and has delivered a genuine transformation at Business School Lausanne. The model is also transferable and can be deployed as an influential alternative vehicle for all public debate and problem solving. This approach will surely become the new normal for transformation management.

A key theme, right through this edition concerns the fundamental question, *what is the purpose of business?* So, it is fitting that we round off this collection with a living example of a major global business that is reinventing itself—to put *real purpose* at the heart of its business strategy. Gabi Zedlmayer, Vice President and Chief Progress Officer, HP shares how HP has embraced this opportunity, in recognition that integrating purpose is essential, not only for society, but also for long-term business growth and the transition to a sustainable economy. Zedlmayer explores how putting purpose at the heart of strategy inspires companies to think differently about innovation; to reach beyond incremental improvements to create transformative solutions; to confront biases and constraints that obscure possibilities; and to connect customer needs with human, economic and environmental impact. The results can be game-changing.

On behalf of everyone that has worked on this *Special Edition of the BSL Journal*, and on the Sustainable Economy Project, itself, I hope you find something of real interest here, and something you can take with you into your own realm of influence, towards a sustainable economy.

I would like to offer my sincere gratitude for the opportunity to work on this collection, shared by Professor Katrin Muff, the Dean of Business School Lausanne. The *BSL Journal* provides an ideal space for us to create a real melting pot of progressive thinking, from some of the leading players in the often separate worlds of business and academia. Enabling collaboration across these boundaries will be so important in making real change happen in our world—and so I commend the great approach that Katrin and her team at BSL are advocating. Please read and enjoy.

Mike Townsend,
Copenhagen, January 2015

Redefining Business Purpose
Driving Societal and Systems Transformation

Paul Polman
CEO Unilever

The world has always faced challenges, but never so many at once: rising unemployment, poverty, food security, climate change, geopolitical instability. Our economic system is not working for everyone. Inequality is rising. Note the recent report from Oxfam, which suggested that by 2016 the wealthiest 1% would own 50% of the world's wealth. On top of that, the population is expected to grow by another 30% by 2050, putting even more strain on our planet and its finite resources. 2015 can be the year when the world fights back. We have the unique opportunity to be the first generation to bring an end to poverty and the last to prevent the worst impacts of climate change. For me, it is a business as well as a moral issue. You can't have a healthy business in a broken world. Business can – and must – be part of the solution to these challenges.

At Unilever, we are pioneering a model that puts addressing the world's challenges at the heart of our business operations and corporate strategy. But we need to work with others to achieve the scale that's needed to help solve such big and pressing issues. We do that on behalf of the people who live in poverty, or are too hungry to go to school, those who may not even have made it beyond the age of five due to malnutrition, natural disasters, or simply poor sanitation.

Later this year, world leaders will meet to agree a new development agenda and a binding climate deal. The outcomes will decide the lives of many. I urge people not to stand at the sidelines – but to get involved and work together. The stakes could hardly be higher. This is a once-in-a-lifetime opportunity. We have to grasp it, and business must be at the centre of the debate.

- Unilever sustainable living plan
- Purpose driven brands
- Human development & climate change
- Transform markets
- Partnerships
- Deforestation

Paul Polman has been Chief Executive Officer of Unilever since 1st January 2009. Under his leadership, Unilever has set out an ambitious vision to double its size, while reducing its overall environmental footprint and increasing its positive social impact. Paul is Chairman of the World Business Council for Sustainable Development, a member of the International Business Council of the World Economic Forum, and serves on the Board of the UN Global Compact. He is also on the Board of the Global Consumer Goods Forum. Paul's contribution to sustainable business and addressing global issues has been well recognized. For example, he is a former recipient of the Atlantic Council Award for Distinguished Business Leadership and the CK Prahalad Award for Global Sustainability Leadership. Last year he received the UN Foundation 'Champion of Global Change' Award. Married with three children, Paul is a former Chairman of Perkins School for the Blind International Advisory Board and serves as President of the Kilimanjaro Blind Trust.

www.unilever.com;
www.projectsunlight.com

A growing threat

The world faces enormous human development and environmental challenges, from poverty and disease to food security and climate change. Significant progress has been made in the last two decades—extreme poverty has halved, hunger has reduced and over 2 billion people have improved access to drinking water (United Nations, 2014).

But huge problems remain. Inequality has widened, one in eight people still go to bed hungry and climate change threatens everything we have achieved since the 1960s. Half a century of progress stands to be wiped out within a generation.

For too long business has sat on the sidelines, either unable or unwilling to be part of the solution to these systemic challenges. But this is now rapidly changing as the limitations of governments and international bodies to resolve them become ever more apparent, as consumers increasingly are demanding change, and as the cost of inaction starts to exceed the cost of action.

The cost of climate change is already high and increasing. The UN Secretary-General has calculated that, since 2000, economic losses from natural disasters total around US$2.5 trillion (United Nations, 2013). The OECD predicts that, by 2050, over US$45 trillion of assets could be at risk from flooding (OECD, 2013). Accenture has found that significant supply chain disruptions can cut the share price of companies by 7% (Risk Response Network and Accenture, 2013), while KPMG estimates that the total profit of the food industry is at risk by 2030.

We are seeing the effect of climate change in our own business. Shipping routes cancelled because of hurricanes in the Philippines. Factories closing because of extreme cold weather in the United States. Distribution networks in disarray because of floods in the UK. Reduced productivity on our tea plantations in Kenya because of weather changes linked to deforestation of the Mau forest. We estimate that geo-political and climate-related factors cost Unilever currently up to €300 million a year. This not only impacts our shareholders but with over 5 million in our supply chain and more than 2 billion consumers around the world, the repercussions ripple much wider.

As tackling these issues becomes not just a moral but a commercial imperative, a growing number of businesses are stepping up to the plate. Today, three-quarters of the largest companies have set themselves clear social and environmental goals, 4000 now report on CO_2 emissions, and 50 of the top 200 have set an internal price for carbon.

The Unilever Sustainable Living Plan

Our own response is set out in the Unilever Sustainable Living Plan, which has set stretching goals to reduce our environmental footprint and increase our social impact as we grow our business. We are making progress. All of the electricity for our sites in North America and Europe now comes from certified, renewable sources. In absolute terms, CO_2 emissions from energy in manufacturing are nearly a third below 2008 levels, water abstraction is down 29% and total waste sent for disposal is down two-thirds—all achieved while increasing production volume. It is making us a more efficient organisation and saving us money—over €300 million in cumulative avoided supply chain costs since 2008.

However, as combating climate change becomes more urgent, the time has come to look beyond incremental reductions in environmental impacts and increases in social impacts, important though these are. Business can and must make a bigger difference to global challenges by leveraging its scale, influence, expertise and resources to drive transformational change at a systemic level.

This is crucial because the economic system we all live and work within drives our behaviours and choices, and without changing them we cannot hope to achieve the structural shifts that have to be made. Business is responsible for more than half the world's GDP, so unless we make change happen, we will not see the reduction in greenhouse gas emissions (GHG) the world needs.

The *Better Growth, Better Climate* report, published in 2014 by the Global Commission on the Economy and Climate, of which I was a member, identified three key systems of the economy where there is huge potential to invest in structural and technological change: cities, which generate around 80% of global output and 70% of global energy use and related GHG emissions; energy systems, where renewables and energy efficiency offer significant investment opportunities; and land use. Food production can be increased and land use emissions cut through more sustainable agricultural practices and by protecting forests from further destruction.

Over half of Unilever's raw materials come from farms and forests. That is why we have committed to work with others and to champion sustainable agriculture in areas where we have most influence, to help smallholder farmers to improve their farming practices and livelihoods, and to eliminate deforestation from supply chains.

We also make and market some of the world's leading personal hygiene and household cleaning products, so we have also committed to help provide good hygiene, safe drinking water and better sanitation for the millions of people around the world who are still denied these basic human rights. All three commitments are directly relevant to our business. All three respond to pressing societal needs.

This is not about mitigation. It is about opportunity and aligning our purpose in business with this opportunity. This is the message the World Business Council for Sustainable Development is championing with its Action 2020 roadmap, which sets out the business agenda for action. It is also one of the key findings of the *Better Growth, Better Climate* report, which argues that traditional macroeconomic objectives are now best achieved through a decisive shift to a new climate economy, with inclusive, high-quality, climate-resilient growth. Although the shift will not be easy, it provides all business sectors with new opportunities to grow.

This is certainly our experience at Unilever. Looking at the world through a sustainability lens not only helps us 'future proof' our supply chain, it also fuels innovation and drives brand growth. Half our agricultural raw materials now come from sustainable sources and we are on track to make that 100% by 2020.[1] Our brands with a strong social purpose, such as Pureit water purifiers, Domestos toilet cleaner and Lifebuoy soap, are not only improving millions of lives by helping to tackle the water, sanitation and hygiene (WASH) agenda. All three achieved double-digit sales growth on average over the past three years. This shows that there doesn't have to be a trade-off between doing well and doing good. On the contrary, purpose-driven brands are growing ahead of the market.

The same is true of brands that reduce environmental impacts. A laundry fabric conditioner that reduces the water needed to rinse clothes by two-thirds, dry shampoos that reduce CO_2 by around 90% compared with washing hair with heated water, ice creams that stay frozen at higher temperatures, and compressed deodorant aerosol sprays with half the propellant gas and 25% less aluminium, are just some of the sustainability-inspired innovations that are growing our business.

These do not just come about because our brand managers have built sustainability into their brand development strategies or our R&D scientists have inserted it into their innovation processes. Everyone who works at Unilever is aware of our Sustainable Living Plan goals and understands the importance of this agenda. This is about bringing the challenges of the outside world into the business, making our employees more conscious of the issues and trends that affect our business, and being more open to ideas that push the boundaries of what we do or come from less conventional sources.

---

1 Our approach and standards are set out in the Unilever Sustainable Agricultural Code.

Making 2015 a year of change

2015 can be a pivotal year for human development and climate change. In September leaders gather in New York to agree the Sustainable Development Goals that will replace the Millennium Development Goals.

The MDGs have made progress in a number of areas but many challenges remain. As Oxfam's report *Wealth: Having It All and Wanting More* has highlighted, levels of inequality are greater than they have ever been, extreme poverty and hunger still afflict more than 800 million people, and pressures on the planet's resources continue to grow.

The SDGs include ending poverty and hunger, reducing inequality and combating climate change as core goals, achievable by 2030. The SDGs are an agenda for everyone, not just the development community, and will require collaboration across all actors in society. The decision by Secretary-General Ban Ki-Moon to invite me to represent the business community on his High Level Panel to advise on the post-2015 development framework is a mark of the importance the UN attaches to the role of the private sector in co-delivering this agenda.

Illustration: Klaus Elle

Then in December, the COP 21 Climate Change Conference in Paris holds out the very real prospect of a global agreement on curbing carbon emissions and the promise of a more stable and sustainable future.

Although run as separate agendas, these two issues—climate and development—are entirely interdependent. We cannot eliminate poverty without enabling developing countries to engage more people in economic activity that uses natural resources, and we cannot resolve runaway climate change without creating wealth in a more equitable and less carbon-intensive way. Left unchecked, climate change risks not only making the poorest poorer, but pulling the emerging middle classes back into poverty too.

Therefore, 2015 is a critical year. As Lord Stern has said, this year will shape the next 20 years and the next 20 years will shape the century. Whatever governments agree to in New York and Paris, and however high or low their level of ambition proves to be, the reality is that these agreements will succeed or fail by how they are implemented by business on the ground. Business as usual is not an option. We have to find new ways of working and new ways of collaborating to bring about real and lasting change.

Partnerships and collaboration will be key

These new approaches require business leaders with different mindsets and capabilities—men and women who can successfully build cross-sector coalitions, who are as familiar dealing with NGOs and policymakers as they are with customers and suppliers, and who are comfortable operating in a more volatile and complex environment. There are no blueprints for how to do this or roadmaps on how to navigate our way towards this brave new world. There is a role management education must play in preparing the business world for a more collaborative future.

I believe the solution is in bringing together the few key players that can make the biggest difference to create the market conditions that can lead to tipping points. It only takes a handful of companies to change together to trigger others to follow and transform whole markets.

This has been the thinking behind Unilever's commitment to play a leading role in helping to end deforestation linked to supply chains. According to the IPCC, deforestation accounts for up to 15% of global greenhouse gas emissions, making it one of the largest contributors to climate change. More than 1.6 billion people worldwide depend directly on forests for food, medicines and fuel, including 60 million indigenous people who are almost entirely dependent on forests for their lives and livelihoods.

Palm oil, a key cause of deforestation, is an important and versatile ingredient found in 50% of all consumer goods. Multinational companies account for around 20% of all palm oil purchases. That is why, in 2010, all 400 members of the global Consumer Goods Forum (CGF) pledged to help achieve zero net deforestation by 2020. The CGF includes all the world's major consumer goods companies, representing about 5% of global GDP. This has accelerated the number of companies committed to buying 100% sustainable palm oil by 2020 or sooner.

This led us to launch the Tropical Forest Alliance at Rio+20 in 2012, a partnership between the CGF and six governments, including Indonesia, a major producer of palm oil, the US and the UK. This in turn led to the New York Declaration on Forests, which took centre stage at the UN Climate Change Conference in September 2014, at which over 170 entities signed up to halving deforestation by 2020 and ending it by 2030.

This new pledge was the first time in history that a critical mass of developed and developing country world leaders partnered around such a goal, which also includes a commitment to restore hundreds of millions of hectares of forest land. Today, with pledges from all the major palm oil producers and most of the world's big manufacturers and retailers, over 70% of the world's globally traded palm oil is now committed to be sustainably sourced. Plantations under commitments cover an area the size of Portugal and the resulting saving to the planet is an estimated reduction of 400–450 million tonnes of carbon dioxide by 2020.

While these organisations still have to deliver on their commitments—so far only 18% of palm oil produced is certified sustainable—this shows what companies, governments and civil society can achieve if we align our efforts behind common goals to achieve transformative change.

If the consumer goods sector can do this with deforestation, just think of the difference that could be made if other sectors convene similar coalitions to drive sustainable practices in other commodity supply chains and with other sources of greenhouse gas emissions.

I am optimistic. Momentum is building. Progress is being made. By changing the way we do business, by seeing the transformation to a low-carbon economy as an opportunity to be seized, not a risk to be managed, by looking beyond our own impacts to systemic areas where we can make a transformational difference, and by working with others to achieve shared goals, business can play a much bigger role in helping to create a better future.

But there's no time to lose. The time to act is now.

References

OECD (2013), *Water Security for Better Lives*, OECD, Paris.

Risk Response Network and Accenture (2013), *Building Resilience in Supply Chains*, World Economic Forum, Geneva.

United Nations (2013), UN Office for Disaster Risk Reduction, Geneva.

United Nations (2014), *The Millennium Development Goals Report 2014*, United Nations, New York.

Doing Business in a Well-Being Economy

Isabel Sebastian

Institute for Sustainable Futures, University of Technology, Sydney, Australia

This article explores business sustainability and CSR in light of research on well-being and happiness, and Bhutan's New Development Paradigm as a model for leveraging change towards a well-being economy. Key implications for business emerging from a literature review and interviews with business and government leaders in Bhutan and across the world are grounded in the author's professional experience in business sustainability. A deep understanding of how well-being can be evaluated in three distinct ways potentially provides a new perspective on the old economic paradigm assumption that humanity is driven by insatiable material wants. This has profound implications challenging business to consider its purpose in the context of an economy that values well-being of its people across multiple dimensions, not only material well-being. Mapping the synergy between leverage points for systemic change and Bhutan's New Development Paradigm reveals that changing measures of success is only one lever out of many and possibly not enough by itself to shift economic paradigms. Three starting points in core business activities are offered as practical examples for applying this research. Ultimately though, businesses aspiring to operate in a well-being economy have to be willing to look for opportunities beyond fulfilling humanity's immediate material needs to shape a world of prosperity and true happiness for all.

- Well-being
- New Economic Paradigm
- Human Needs
- Life Satisfaction
- Business Purpose
- CSR

Isabel has worked in travel, tourism and boutique hotels for the majority of her 20-year career. Her experience spans from Europe to Asia and Australia specialising in sustainable business operations and well-being outcomes within management, strategic planning, teaching and consulting roles. She has worked in travel & tour companies, airlines, industry associations, NGOs, universities, boutique hotels and as a director of her sustainable tourism consultancy in Australia. For the past eight years she worked in Bhutan, implementing a 'beyond CSR' project, incorporating the principles of Gross National Happiness (GNH) during 2010/11. She is currently undertaking a PhD at the Institute for Sustainable Futures, University of Technology Sydney, and has been an Associate at the Environment and Sustainability Institute at Exeter University between Dec 2015 and March 2015.

✉ Institute for Sustainable Futures, University of Technology Sydney, PO Box 123, Broadway, NSW 2007, Australia

🖥 Isabel.Sebastian@uts.edu.au

☎ +61 2 9514 4950

Is corporate social responsibility (CSR) enough in a new economy?

> shifting a system such as the economy requires simultaneous action on a number of leverage points by a critical mass of the system's stakeholders

Many of the genuine CSR and corporate sustainability champions have pushed sustainability performance a long way towards doing less harm and contributing more to society and nature through their business activities. However, these efforts have not consistently delivered more sustainable outcomes for the economy, society and the environment (Windsor, 2012; Kemper & Martin 2010). Part of the reason for this is that shifting a system such as the economy requires simultaneous action on a number of leverage points by a critical mass of the system's stakeholders.

When political leaders speak of Well-being Economics (APPGWE 2014) and business leaders speak of Human Economies (Seidman 2014) they describe the leverage points and transformation necessary to address the ecological and social challenges of a globalised world. Even the most challenging conversation that goes to the very heart of the purpose of business in society is emerging in the business sector—the conundrum of infinite economic growth on a planet with finite resources (Miller, 2013). Phillipe Joubert, Senior Adviser to the World Business Council for Sustainable Development points out that 'business as usual is no longer possible' (Benson, 2012) and that business innovation and ingenuity needs to turn to designing new business models to support a new economic system.

There are a string of other terms being used interchangeably and with overlapping ideas to describe a new style of economy that is more sustainable and equitable than the current system. Prefixes to the term 'economy' or economics attempt to describe this phenomenon, such as welfare (Pigou et al. 2013), sustainable (Meadows & Club of Rome. 1972); green (Pearce et al. 1989); human (Hart et al. 2010); ethical (Arvidsson, 2008); well-being (APPGWE, 2014); Darwin (Frank, 2011); conscious (Mackey & Sisodia, 2013); common good (Daly et al. 1989; Felber 2010) and many more. Particularly since the most recent economic crisis there is a noticeable increase in ideas on how to transition to a new economic order. Critics point out that these ideas of a new economic system are unrealistic and would threaten economies to collapse (Fürst 2011; Ben-Ami 2010). However, at the same time there is a rising interest from business leaders and entrepreneurs to ready themselves for an economy where measures of progress go beyond purely material well-being. No one wants economic collapse or to lose the standard of living they are used to. New economic thinking and models contribute a wide range of systems solutions to avoid collapse and suffering. Therefore, the question whether CSR can prepare business for re-imagining its business model in a new economic order may be provocative, but now could be the time to ask it. When thinking of new strategy, new customers and new markets, new economic thinking has to stretch to include new measures of success, such as happiness and well-being and the core of business purpose. If CSR and sustainability activities are able to influence the core of a business's purpose then they may be the perfect stepping stone towards new economic thinking. However, if they are considered a burden, obligation or marketing tool they may not be able to provide a platform for systems change.

> If CSR and sustainability activities are able to influence the core of a business's purpose then they may be the perfect stepping stone towards new economic thinking. However, if they are considered a burden, obligation or marketing tool they may not be able to provide a platform for systems change

Happiness in economic thought

The pursuit of happiness in economics clearly matters as defined in the term 'utility' (Bentham, 1789). It refers to the benefit that a person experiences from consuming goods and services. The economics discipline traditionally assumes that the satisfaction of a person is determined by their consumption of goods and services, creating a tension between limited resources and the unlimited wants of humankind. However, consumer demand theory does recognise the 'law of diminishing marginal utility' (Jevons, 1866) as the threshold of satisfaction after which consumption will no longer bring pleasure. In other words, the total benefit and pleasure derived from more consumption will increase at a slower and slower rate until it declines, the more a person consumes of a particular product or service. This process is also referred to in psychology as adaptation (Diener et al. 2006) or a balancing feedback loop in systems-theory (Meadows, 2008). The challenge of measuring the subjective and ever-changing levels of satisfaction derived from consumption then is solved in the field of economics by observing the consumption choices people make, revealing their ultimate preferences (Frey and Stutzer 2001). Economics assumes that humans are rational, predictable and that their preferences are the foremost indication to judge their relative happiness.

Most business models are based on fulfilling the seemingly unlimited wants of humankind often forgetting or ignoring the fact that the actual benefit and pleasure will decrease with more consumption. It is here that the last 40 years of research into happiness and well-being starts to illuminate the dead-end that consumption beyond basic needs presents when it comes to finding lasting contentment, happiness and well-being.

> the last 40 years of research into happiness and well-being starts to illuminate the dead-end that consumption beyond basic needs presents when it comes to finding lasting contentment, happiness and well-being

What do we know about happiness and well-being?

Happiness and well-being research offers a new dimension for understanding the economic system, people's behaviours, choices and perceived sense of well-being. Over the past 40 years, disciplines ranging from psychology to neuroscience and from economics to business science, just to name a few, have been researching what makes humans and societies happy and well. One of the early thoughts in Western philosophy on happiness dates back to Aristotle's idea of *eudemonia,* interpreted as 'the good life', 'flourishing' or living a 'life with purpose' for the highest human good, where happiness is not only about how a person feels but also about what a person does (Alipour *et al.*, 2012). There is still much debate about definitions of happiness and subjective well-being, the difference between the two, the causal relationships between happiness and its drivers such as income, and whether it can be measured reliably or not (Easterlin 1974; Diener 1984; Kahneman & Krueger, 2006; Veenhoven & Hagerty, 2006; Seligman, 2011). '...It is apparent from much of the scientific literature that well-being is a complex and contestable construct and that, despite intense academic scrutiny and a voluminous literature, its definition remains unresolved' (Carlisle *et al.* 2009).

While there is still no agreement on definitions of happiness and well-being, there seems to have been some alignment particularly in the last three years about how to measure those phenomena (Kahneman & Deaton 2010). This in itself potentially implies that there has to be some agreement on how positive emotions, life satisfaction and a sense of meaning in life are comprised in the concept of well-being.

The underlying assumption to all of this research seems to be the fact that every human being is motivated by the search for happiness with many considering it a given right (McMahon, 2007). Happiness research therefore now provides much fuel to inform the 'beyond GDP' debate (European Commission, 2013), which has inspired new measures of progress, policies, theories and indicators of sustainable development and well-being in many countries across the world (Hák *et al.* 2012).

These indicators describe, rather than define what contributes to happiness and well-being. Some examples of indicators and theories on what contributes to happiness have emerged from:

▶ Authors such as Richard Layard (2005), Martin Seligman (2011), Daniel Kahneman (2011) and Paul Dolan (2014)

▶ Government initiatives such as Bhutan's Gross National Happiness (GNH) Index (Ura *et al.* 2012), Office for National Statistics UK 'National Well-being: Measuring what matters' (2014) and the OECD's Better Life Index (2013)

▶ Community initiatives such as the Australian National Development Index (Salvaris, 2013) and NGO initiatives such as the Legatum Prosperity Index (Legatum, 2014), New Economics Foundation's Happy Planet Index, and academic initiatives such as the Social Progress Imperative's Social Progress Index

A comparison of the determinants of happiness and well-being from these sources and the literature reveals a set of 11 key areas of life that are considered vital contributing factors to happiness and well-being as shown in Figure 1.

Figure 1 Determinants of happiness and well-being

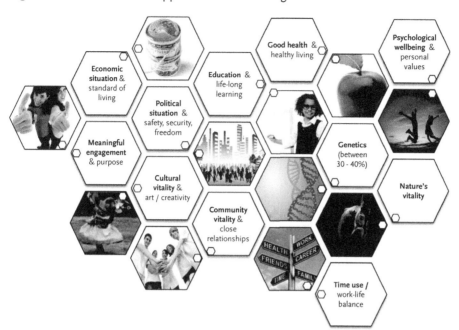

For the purpose of this article, the determinant of 'Economic Situation & Standard of Living' is of particular interest since this is where business currently plays a major role in fulfilling material needs of people and societies. There are a number of key insights from happiness and well-being research in relation to standard of living that provide important insights for business:

▷ Income increases levels of happiness up to a certain point, beyond which people adjust their expectations and it does not improve subjective well-being (Easterlin, 1995; Diener and Seligman, 2004; Clark *et al.* 2008)

▷ Studies in the US have found the threshold where the happiness derived from more income diminishes at around US$75,000 income per year (Kahneman & Deaton 2010)

▷ Social comparison means that in any society rich people are happier than poor people, but over time richer societies are no happier than poorer ones (Layard, 2005; Graham 2009)

▷ People compare themselves to others close by (reference group) and adjust expectations of how much income generates happiness (Easterlin, 2003)

▷ The process of adapting to higher standards of living results in more consumption in an attempt to experience more satisfaction and happiness. In other words we are caught on a 'hedonic treadmill' (Brickman and Campbell, 1971) that inevitably brings us back to a happiness set-point (Headey, 2006)

▶ Global GDP has increased by 300% since 1950; however global genuine progress per capita as measured by Genuine Progress Indicator peaked in 1978. A study comparing life satisfaction in 17 countries from 1950 to 2003 shows no significant improvements since 1975 (Kubiszewski *et al.* 2013). This is also called the 'threshold point beyond which, if there is more economic growth, quality of life may begin to deteriorate' (Max-Neef, 1995)

Not only what we measure determines what we do

The pursuit of improving the quality of life and well-being for a large proportion of the global population has driven much of human activity and ingenuity, particularly over the last 100 years. This pursuit has established economic growth as the key measure of success of human industriousness, productivity and nations. The measure of Gross National Product (GNP) developed by Kuznets (1934) allows consistent comparison of the amount of effort that is expended in an economy regardless of whether this effort improves or deteriorates societal well-being. Kuznets himself warned that this measure should not be mistaken as a barometer of societal well-being or to determine social policy. In his words 'the welfare of a nation can scarcely be inferred from a measurement of national income' (European Commission, 2013). Despite his warnings, GNP (or GDP) was adopted by most nations from hereon as their measure of economic progress and for the purpose of comparison between each other. Economist and Nobel Laureate Joseph Stiglitz (2009) said that 'in a performance based society, what we measure determines what we do and if we measure the wrong thing, we do the wrong thing.'

> **Changing the success measure of an economy would clearly be a game-changer, somewhat like changing the rules of a Monopoly game from the winner being the one with most property to the one who managed to establish the most communities with optimal well-being and life satisfaction**

The current economic, environmental and societal difficulties that the globalised world and humanity find themselves in seem adequate proof for Stiglitz's assertion. Changing the success measure of an economy would clearly be a game-changer, somewhat like changing the rules of a Monopoly game from the winner being the one with most property to the one who managed to establish the most communities with optimal well-being and life satisfaction. Changing the rules of a game requires willingness and interest of the players, just like changing the measures of progress requires politicians, business leaders and societies to want to see the world through a new lens. This willingness, however, depends on the other variable mentioned by Stiglitz— our competition and performance mindsets. Some argue it is human nature to compete for survival and others argue that cooperation and altruism are just as common in evolution (Ridley

2003). Either way, important recent findings from neuroscience have shown that the capacity for attitudes and behaviours such as compassion can be taught and learned (Klimecki *et al.* 2014; Leiberg *et al.* 2011) just like competitive behaviour can be learned. Research findings relating to neuroplasticity in adult brains therefore provide some of the most promising opportunities for those genuinely committed to empowering individuals and societies to create economies that are dedicated to well-being. Therefore, this raises the question of what it will take for all the players in the economy, particularly business, to move towards promoting all dimensions of well-being as the winning game rather than just material well-being.

> **this raises the question of what it will take for all the players in the economy, particularly business, to move towards promoting all dimensions of well-being as the winning game rather than just material well-being**

While more voices are emerging from among policy, economic, academic and business thinkers, promoting new indicators of progress beyond GDP to include well-being as a key aim or even as an over-arching societal aim (European Commission, 2013; National Research Council, 2013; NDP, 2013; O'Donnell 2014), there are only a few that call for a shift of mindsets, willingness and paradigms through a new narrative for a new economy (Korten & Scharmer 2014).

The extensive focus on the many new measures of progress and prosperity has resulted at least in some agreement about measuring the different dimensions of what is now called 'subjective well-being' (Kahneman and Deaton, 2010; National Research Council, 2013; OECD, 2013).

There are three distinct aspects of subjective well-being recognised as providing reliable evaluation of happiness and well-being:

1. **Life satisfaction or evaluative well-being** measures how people think about their life overall considering past events, opportunities and outcomes up to the present

2. **Emotional or experienced well-being** measures the frequency and intensity of emotions experienced by an individual on a day to day basis looking at immediate present experience of pleasant or unpleasant emotions (also called 'hedonic' well-being)

3. **Life purpose and meaning** measures the outlook looking more towards the future at a person's sense of contribution and engagement (also called 'eudemonic' well-being)

For the purpose of this article I will be referring to these three ways of experiencing well-being and happiness that otherwise could have conflicting and overlapping meanings. Figure 2 is an attempt at a visual representation of how the vast empirical and theoretical body of research on assessing happiness and well-being could be viewed in context. It also includes an example of the questions that might be asked to assess the three expressions of happiness and well-being. It is, however, important to note that most research that measures well-being and happiness will incorporate a substantial set of questions under each of these three categories.

Figure 2 Three dimensions of measuring subjective well-being

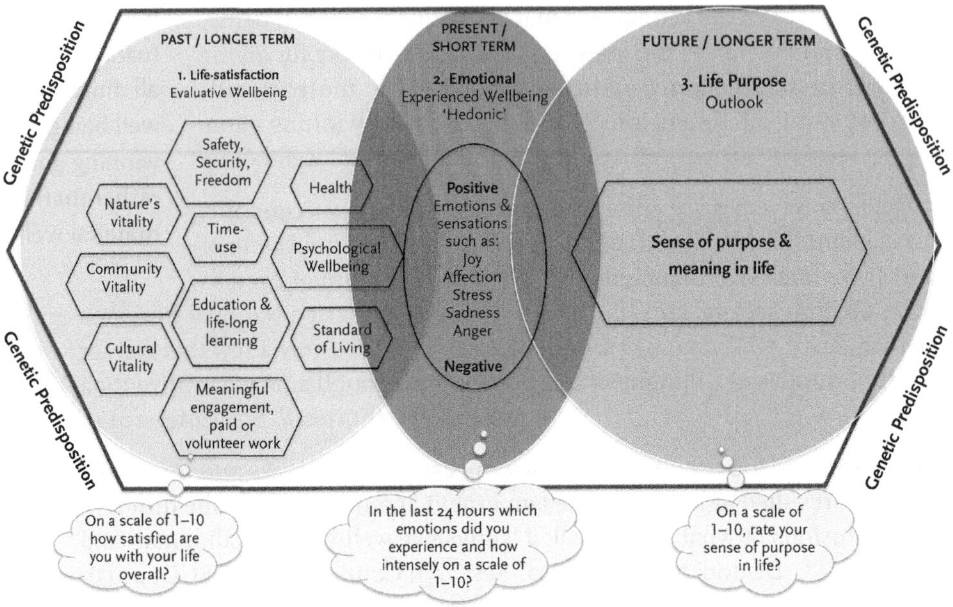

While genetic predisposition is said to account for 30–40% of variation in happiness levels (De Neve *et al.*, 2012; Lykken & Tellegen, 1996, Rietveld *et al.* 2013), there is another 60–70% that can be influenced through other external influences and internal capabilities. Therefore the choices, behaviours, thoughts and actions in the present will have a large impact on how we evaluate our life satisfaction overall and will also set the stage for how we evaluate future outlook on life. At the same time our evaluation of our life satisfaction and outlook on life can also influence our present emotional experience. In other words, they can both be the cause, effect and condition of a present emotional state. The only influence we have over our lives though are the choices, behaviours, thoughts and actions that we express and exert in the present moment. Therefore it is of crucial importance to understand the interconnectedness of past, present and future perceptions of well-being and happiness. The tremendous implications for business when evaluating well-being in this way are explored in the later section of this article.

A new development paradigm: a perspective from Bhutan

An interesting approach to development and progress is practised in Bhutan where the government sets societal well-being as its over-arching aim to guide all government activities within the country. His Majesty, the 4th King of Bhutan articulated this approach in 1976, when he famously declared that 'Gross National Happiness is more important than Gross National Product' (GNH Centre, 2013). Initially, the statement provided an intuitive guiding principle; however over the past 10 years two tools for operationalising GNH have been developed—the GNH Index (Ura *et al.* 2012) and a GNH policy-screening tool. A set of 33 indicators provide a deep insight into the state of the nation through Bhutanese perceptions and satisfaction across the nine domains of education, environmental conservation, standard of living, community vitality, time-use, good governance, health, psychological well-being and cultural preservation. The Bhutanese government uses the policy-screening tool to ensure that only policies are implemented that enhance or at least do not weaken the GNH Index. The difference in Bhutan compared with other countries that are now measuring or promoting the use of well-being indicators is that both GNH tools are actively being used by Bhutan's government as a compass for decision-making on budget allocations and programmes. A wide range of research has been published on the measurement approach of the GNH index (Helliwell *et al.* 2012; Ura *et al.*, 2012) and its application in policy decision-making (Martin, 2012); however very little research has explored the impact of a GNH or well-being economy on the business sector.

> The difference in Bhutan compared with other countries that are now measuring or promoting the use of well-being indicators is that both GNH tools are actively being used by Bhutan's government as a compass for decision-making on budget allocations and programmes

Commissioned by the United Nations, over the past two years Bhutan coordinated an international trans-disciplinary working group of some 70 experts spanning all fields of science including leading academics and thought leaders such as David Suzuki, Martin Seligman and Tim Jackson to mention just a few (NDP, 2013). The aim was to develop a New Development Paradigm (NDP) framework that would support global development with the central purpose of societal well-being. Figure 3 is an adapted version of the NDP framework highlighting how this model is currently being implemented in Bhutan.

Figure 3 Adapted version of the 'New Development Paradigm'

Source: *Towards a New Development Paradigm* report by the Government of Bhutan (NDP 2013)

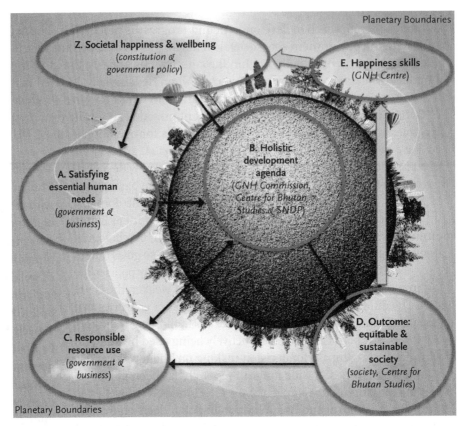

As highlighted in Figure 3, the NDP framework places 'Societal Happiness and Well-being' as the ultimate goal of all development and progress and is based on two fundamental assumptions (NDP, 2013) that:

▶ The universal human goal to pursue well-being and happiness is not just a private or individual goal but a societal vision

▶ Planetary boundaries exist and that there are severe ecological realities that require a recalibration of current development activities

The framework brings together a new paradigm and solutions from across the world, with the UN vision and global commitments, and Bhutan's experience of aiming for GNH. The framework as proposed by the international working group adopts well-known principles of sustainable development, balancing economic, social and environmental concerns (box B), promoting responsible resource use (box C) and measurement of well-being indicators (box D) to ensure that any development improves societal well-being (box Z) across all domains. Of most interest though are two new dimensions, previously unseen in sustainable development models, which reveal the very essence of a well-being economy. First, the distinction between the long-term needs for a satisfying life versus the insatiable short-term needs (box A) provides a window of opportunity to promote the understanding of the multiple dimensions of well-being across global societies. Second is the acknowledgement that creating the conditions for sustainability and measuring societal happiness and well-being by themselves are not enough when the aim is societal well-being. The NDP model proposes that the opportunity for every person to pursue their full human potential requires that they are able to acquire the knowledge, skills and ability for self-actualisation and skilful emotion management or emotional intelligence described as 'happiness skills' (box E). This claim is supported by the research that shows that skills like compassion and happiness can be learned (Leiberg *et al.*, 2011; Ricard 2006). The NDP model therefore provides new perspectives not only on new measures of progress and success but more importantly it highlights the role and opportunity of each individual person in creating systems change.

> **The NDP model therefore provides new perspectives not only on new measures of progress and success but more importantly it highlights the role and opportunity of each individual person in creating systems change.**

The NDP framework was submitted to the UN post-2015 consultative process as a contribution to the formulation of a new set of sustainable development goals, which will be released in 2015.

Levers for systemic change

Interestingly the NDP framework displays key components identified by Meadows (1999, 2008) as effective levers for creating systemic change. According to Meadows (2009), creating change in a dynamic system means finding the most effective leverage points to push, as they are the most powerful places to intervene in a system. They are the points where small changes have the potential to lead to large shifts in behaviour and the dynamics of an entire system (Meadows, 2009). According to Forrester (1971), evidence suggests that the people who are deeply immersed in organisational and structural systems (such as governments or the financial and money sectors) often intuitively know where to find those points of power, but most of the time they push change in the wrong direction.

Meadows (2009) asserts that world leaders are rightly obsessed with economic growth as the answer to virtually all problems; however 'they are pushing with all their might in the wrong direction'. As Forrester (1971) found in his studies of systems dynamics, complex systems are often counterintuitive, resulting in their leverage points being not what one would expect. Therefore, these leverage points are often used backward, which causes an existing problem to be systematically worsened rather than being solved (Meadows, 2009). The worsening global financial, social and environmental crisis could be evidence of this systemic worsening due to the direction of change applied to leverage points by policy makers and business leaders over the last 100 years. Hence, the real systems leverage points can often seem incredibly obscure, frustratingly subtle and very surprising. A key question is whether the NDP model, with its goal as societal happiness and well-being, could be one of those powerful counterintuitive leverage points to use?

Meadows (1999) proposed a 12-point scale to evaluate the effectiveness of leverage points in complex systems. Table 1 outlines a condensed version of the scale as six leverage categories. Meadows (1999) suggests that 'changing measurements and parameters' is a lower order leverage point compared to shifting mindsets and being able to let go of out-dated perspectives. She proposes that 'transcending paradigms' is the most powerful leverage point to create a shift in complex systems. However, the most powerful leverage point also introduces major uncertainty, complexity and potentially chaos that may be beyond human comprehension and would require relinquishing some of the control over the system.

> **working at the highest level of systems change requires individual transformation and mastery, or in other words complete willingness to change how we view the world and to let go of old paradigms.**

As Meadows points out, working at the highest level of systems change requires individual transformation and mastery, or in other words complete willingness to change how we view the world and to let go of old paradigms. It requires recognition that our own worldview is a limited understanding of the laws of the universe and that no paradigm reflects the truth and that this in itself is a paradigm. Her profound conclusion is that: In the end, it seems that power has less to do with pushing leverage points than it does with strategically, profoundly, madly letting go! (Meadows, 2009)

Meadows' sentiment is also echoed in the NDP framework highlighting that: The inner transformation of our own mindsets and behaviours is as important for happiness as the transformation of the outer conditions of well-being (NDP, 2013).

Figure 4 Visual representation of the author's interpretation of the relationship between the components of the NDP Model (A, B, C, D, Z) and Meadows' (2009) 12 leverage points (condensed here into six categories, in order of least to most powerful S, T, U, V, W, X)

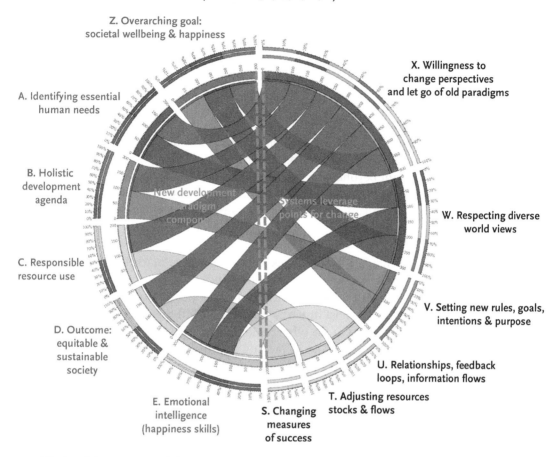

All six of the NDP model components address one of the levers of change, indicating that the NDP model is a well-balanced framework with potential to cause systemic change.

The aim of a well-being economy in light of a New Development Paradigm

The NDP framework provides an interesting lens through which to understand the implications of a well-being economy for the business sector. The aim of a well-being economy in an NDP context would be to:

▷ Avoid the perpetuation of the 'hedonic treadmill' of ever increasing consumption as it has been shown not to improve long-term societal happiness and well-being once a comfortable standard of living has been reached

▷ Ensure that government policy and business strategy work together to provide opportunities, conditions, products and services that empower individuals and societies to understand and cater for all three dimensions of happiness and well-being

▷ Adopt policies and strategies that position improving societal well-being as the most important over-arching national and international goal, and are based on the results of measuring across the three dimensions of subjective well-being

▷ Be alert to recognise the point in economic development when standard of living has reached the optimal level for the majority of people (the point beyond which a higher standard of living does not significantly contribute to increases in well-being) to refocus development and business efforts on long-term life satisfaction instead of further improving the standard of living

Particularly in developed countries, where markets are saturated and consumption is stagnant or declining, educating consumers and engaging them in activities that will enhance overall life satisfaction and life purpose would be the most important paradigm shift that responsible businesses could lead. On the other hand, most developing countries would most likely choose to focus on improving conditions for health, safety and access to food and shelter—primarily improving the standard of living for their citizens. Therefore, economic development policies and business strategies in developing countries would be vastly different from those in developed countries as there will be different starting points and pathways to improving societal well-being.

It is also important to note in this context that the aim of a well-being economy would not be to deny or eliminate the existence of negative emotions. As mentioned in the NDP model under the label of 'happiness skills', a well-being economy is about empowering people with emotional intelligence skills to experience the full range of human emotions and to know how to process and deal with them in a constructive, agile and positive way.

How can business use CSR as a stepping-stone towards well-being economic orientation?

Businesses, ranging from entrepreneurs to multinational companies are the engine of economic activity in most nations across the world. Sudkhedv (2012) suggests that 70% of the global workforce is employed by, and almost 60% of global GDP is generated by, the private business sector. Business is therefore a key stakeholder and at the centre of the transformation that is required to create a systemic shift, from economies that purely grow production and consumption, perpetuating the 'hedonic treadmill' measured through GDP, to growing improved outcomes in societal well-being, quality of life, life satisfaction and engagement with a life purpose.

> **Business is therefore a key stakeholder and at the centre of the transformation that is required to create a systemic shift**

Now more than ever before business has a significant role in creating more responsible economic development and economies. It seems that creating well-being in society through different business models is beginning to receive more attention from business leaders such as Yvonne Chuinard of Patagonia, the late Ray Anderson of Interface, Dov Seidman of LRN, Paul Polman of Unilever, Ian Cheshire of Kingfisher and Tony Hsieh of Zappos.

A shift towards more responsible and holistic business models has been observed with a rising number of companies dedicating their purpose to solving social or environmental problems while being profitable businesses (Haugh, 2005; Leaderbeater, 1997). This shift can also be seen in the fact that some 90% of all Fortune 500 companies now report on their corporate social disclosure (Weber and Marley, 2012). While some see social entrepreneurship as an exciting emerging field (Roberts & Woods, 2005), others posit that there is no 'non-social' business (Seelos & Mair, 2005) and that the original purpose of all business activity was to provide benefits to society and build conditions for societal well-being through employment (Reynolds *et al.* 2002). Either way, business in all its shapes and forms, whether a social enterprise, a CSR champion or a purely self-interested, profit-oriented business, seems to be the gateway to building an economy that fosters all dimensions of well-being for all of its stakeholders.

When overlaying the NDP model with Meadows' (1999) leverage points it becomes apparent that business can be a powerful actor in creating systems change towards a well-being economy. Table 2 provides examples of what businesses that see their role in a well-being economy could do.

Table 1 Some examples of business strategies and activities in a well-being economy (leverage point categories down the left column are listed in order of least effective [6] to most effective [1])

Leverage points / New Development Paradigm components	Z. Overarching goal: societal well-being	A. Identifying genuine human needs	B. Holistic business strategy	C. Responsible Resource Use	D. Outcome: equitable & sustainable society	E. Emotional Intelligence & agility
S. Changing parameters and measures of success	Adopting KPIs that prioritise stakeholder and societal well-being	Clearly differentiating between stakeholders' essential needs and the wants that perpetuate the hedonic treadmill	Measuring business success against a set of holistic objectives and targets	Measuring key environmental, social and human indicators	Measuring well-being indicators of all stakeholders across the 11 determinants	Measuring psychological well-being of all stakeholders
T. Adjusting resource stocks, flows, infrastructure, networks, products and services	Product & Service innovation that is focused on enhancing life satisfaction, psychological well-being and life purpose	Focusing innovation in the areas of the 11 determinants of well-being (see Figure 1)	Investing in infrastructure and resources that offer products and services in the areas of the 11 determinants of well-being	Adopting circular, sharing and collaborative resource practices	Transitioning to offering increasing numbers of products and services that help people fulfil needs within the areas of the 11 determinants of well-being	Providing opportunities for all stakeholders to acquire skills and experience in managing emotions in a skilful and agile way
U. Transparency of relationships, behaviours, feedback loops, information flows	Reporting on the well-being indicators of all business stakeholders across the 3 dimensions outlined in Figure 2	Engaging with all business stakeholders especially customers to understand their genuine needs across the 11 determinants of well-being	Sharing insights with all stakeholders on well-being challenges addressed and outcomes achieved	Rewarding behaviours and communication that respect natural, human and social resources and enhances them rather than depleting them	Encouraging behaviours and communication that respect resources through marketing and public relations	Dealing with integrity, honesty and patience with all stakeholders in the interest of societal well-being

V. Setting new rules, goals, intentions and purpose	Redefining the purpose and vision of a business towards societal well-being	Engaging with all business stakeholders to co-create business purpose and intentions that address any of the 11 determinants of well-being	Organising business strategy around financial, social, environmental and well-being objectives & targets that address any of the 11 determinants of well-being	Setting operating procedures and policies that clearly outline the respectful use of natural, human and social resources in undertaking business activity	Leading by example by forgoing short-term gains for long-term benefits to the business, its stakeholders and society	Empowering all stakeholders to take charge of their psychological well-being to build emotional intelligence and agility
W. Respecting and understanding diverse world views	Promoting industry, national and international dialogue that fosters the exchange of wisdom, insight and compassion	Fulfilling short-term essential needs of stakeholders first and when adequate standard of living is reached then focusing on life satisfaction needs in the 11 areas of well-being	Building tolerance, acceptance and inclusiveness of a wide range of world views through business objectives and strategies	Understanding the positive and negative impacts on natural, human and social resources resulting from business activity	Using emotional intelligence to create shared value of business activity for all stakeholders	Facilitating inter-stakeholder group dialogue to foster awareness, understanding and compassion for a wide range of world views and common goals
X. Willingness and ability to change perspectives and let go of old paradigms	Committing to a new story that measures progress across all 3 dimensions of well-being (see Figure 2) as the most important measure of progress for business and economic activity; recognising GDP growth as a deficient and misleading progress measure	Championing and promoting the difference between the 'hedonic treadmill' style of consumption and the type of consumer engagement that delivers life satisfaction and life purpose	Exploring and considering shared ownership structures	Reinventing the way energy and natural resources are sourced and used, human resources are nurtured and social capital is enhanced through any business activity	Distributing profits, wealth and benefits equitably among stakeholders, solving trade-off conflicts by activating the generosity of those who are better off	Committing to using the power of business with compassion to facilitate all stakeholders to live a deeply satisfying life, grounded in psychological well-being and with a sense of purpose and meaning in life

Where to begin?

While Table 2 provides a full spectrum of examples of the leverage points for businesses wanting to engage in a well-being economy, Table 2 presents three essential starting points.

Table 2 Three essential starting points

From this....	To this....
Market Research	
➤ Researching consumer behaviour and preferences is an extensive field with the purpose of identifying attitudes, needs, wants and decision-making and levels of happiness and satisfaction of consumers. Most of consumer research focuses on how satisfied customers are with products and services, which evaluates the immediate 'experienced' satisfaction or disappointment of a particular product or service;	➤ Redesign consumer research into measuring the well-being and happiness across the three dimensions of subjective well-being. Ideally, this would be done across all stakeholders including employees, suppliers, customers, shareholders and all other stakeholders. This would help businesses to understand if products and services are able to deliver beyond the immediate experienced emotional happiness.
Business Purpose	
➤ Product development and innovation are driven by a business's vision and purpose. Identifying and fulfilling new customer needs and creating new wants therefore is the purpose of most businesses. The great majority of businesses in developed countries focus on fulfilment of needs to evoke an immediate experience of pleasurable emotions and sensations rather than improving overall life satisfaction or life purpose.	➤ Basing product/service development on the results of well-being research that clearly differentiates between the outcomes of overall life satisfaction, experienced happiness and life purpose for all target markets. For example, in developed economies where consumer needs are saturated, demand is stagnant or declining and where consumers are locked in on a 'hedonic treadmill', businesses could focus on any of the 11 determinants that increase 'evaluative' well-being (life satisfaction) or that help improve people's outlook through engagement with a purpose and meaning in life.
Employees and Supply Chain	
➤ While many employers are recognising that happier employees are more productive and higher levels of employee satisfaction and well-being makes organisations more successful, many of the supply chain workers in the globalised economy are suffering.	➤ To ensure that conditions not only within company offices provide the best possible opportunity for employees to improve subjective well-being in all three dimensions, but to ensure supply chain employees and customer outlets provide the same possibility.

The role of business is particularly important as many consumer-oriented businesses are based on perpetuating the 'hedonic treadmill' by simply fulfilling the short-term demands of consumers. This is an important role, when it comes to fulfilling essential needs such as food, shelter, health and safety needs where standards of living are low. However, when overall life satisfaction hardly improves even with ever-increasing living standards it is time for business to engage a different strategy.

> when overall life satisfaction hardly improves even with ever-increasing living standards it is time for business to engage a different strategy.

Illustration: Klaus Elle

If businesses only focus on short-term satisfaction from attempting to increase standards of living beyond the optimal point, humanity will never be able to reach its full potential and life satisfaction. Acknowledged in the 'law of diminishing marginal utility' and the concept of the 'hedonic treadmill', purely focusing on delivering positive emotions in the short-term is likely to perpetuate the current economic paradigm and global crisis. This approach potentially keeps people trapped in a 'consumption-addiction' cycle. While aiming for market saturation makes for a successful business strategy at the moment, it may also be in part responsible for preventing humanity evolving beyond a consumerist society. Companies that keep perpetuating old paradigm thinking, basing their growth strategy on selling more fast-moving consumer goods, are in danger of finding themselves wedded to a losing strategy very soon. Perhaps now is the time to consider recalibrating business growth strategies to growing well-being across the 11 determinants of well-being as outlined in Figure 1 above.

> If businesses only focus on short-term satisfaction from attempting to increase standards of living beyond the optimal point, humanity will never be able to reach its full potential and life satisfaction

> Businesses, their leaders and stakeholders, that are committed to being at the forefront of creating a well-being economy, therefore would need to take some courageous steps beyond CSR strategies

The fact that people can experience high levels of positive emotions but at the same time report low overall life satisfaction and vice versa provides wide ranging opportunities for business to play a role in operating in a well-being economy. Sustainable business practices and CSR excellence provide an important basis of values and intentions within the business sector to contribute to reducing negative impacts of doing business. However, those alone are not enough to steer businesses on a path towards improving societal well-being let alone the well-being of its stakeholders. Businesses, their leaders and stakeholders, that are committed to being at the forefront of creating a well-being economy, therefore would need to take some courageous steps beyond CSR strategies such as:

▶ Raising awareness and understanding in the economy of the difference between short-term experienced happy emotions (hedonic well-being), versus long-term life satisfaction derived from the things that matter in life (the 11 determinants of well-being)

▶ Taking an honest look at the purpose of a business and whether it delivers or supports any of the 11 areas of life that contribute to life satisfaction. If the answer is no, then this may be a good time to plan a transition to new product or service innovations in some of the 11 areas that contribute to long-term well-being and life satisfaction

▶ Exploring the 11 determinants of well-being for new business opportunities with the intention of bringing long-term life satisfaction to societies with a high standard of living and continuing to satisfy essential needs where standards of living are still lagging behind

Conclusion

The progress made by business in CSR and sustainability is testament to the commitment and innovation towards a more sustainable economy. However, for business to be ready to perform in an economy where success is measured by a holistic set of well-being indicators, this will require more from business. It will require a deep understanding of the science of well-being and happiness, an acknowledgement of the interconnectedness of shared responsibility for pushing the right leverage points and the willingness to give up old paradigms.

Too often, a focus on well-being and happiness is considered either as a luxury or trivial. However, especially during hard economic times, when GDP growth is promoted as the only solution, this is the perfect moment to transform our perspectives on what kind of prosperity really matters in life and how we define societies' success. The intention of this article is to challenge the view of GDP growth, both through encouraging businesses and their leaders to explore a new narrative, and by outlining some practical approaches, to growing well-being across its multiple dimensions; thus providing an alternative pathway to building flourishing businesses and deeply satisfied societies in a sustainable economy.

References

Alipour, A., Pedram, A., Abedi, M. and Rostami, Z. (2012) 'What is Happiness?' *Interdisciplinary Journal of Contemporary Research In Business*, 3: 12, pp. 660-667

All-Party Parliamentary Group on Wellbeing Economics (APPGWE) (2014), *Wellbeing in four policy areas*, New Economics Foundation, London, UK

Ben-Ami, D. (2010), *Ferraris for all: In defence for economic progress*, Policy, Bristol; Portland, OR.

Benson, E. (2012), *Corporate leaders, governments and civil society agree that corporate reporting metrics, 'beyond GDP' indicators and the Sustainable Development Goals must be aligned to the same understanding of progress*, media release, Green Economy Coalition, London, viewed 15 May 2013, http://measurewhatmatters.info/wp-content/uploads/2014/01/RIO+20-MEDIA-RELEASE-Measuring-what-matters.pdf.

Bentham, J. (1789) An Introduction to the Principle of Morals and Legislations (1789); reprinted (Oxford, UK: Blackwell, 1948).

Brickman P, Campbell DT. (1971), Hedonic Relativism and Planning the Good Society. In MH Appley (Ed.): 287 – 304

Carlisle, S., Henderson, G. & Hanlon, P.W. (2009), '"Wellbeing": A collateral casualty of modernity?', *Soc Sci Med*, vol. 69, no. 10, pp. 1556-60.

Clark, A.E., Frijters, P. & Shields, M.A. (2008), 'Relative income, happiness, and utility: An explanation for the easterlin paradox and other puzzles', *Journal of Economic Literature*, vol. 46, no. 1, pp. 95-144.

Daly, H.E., Cobb, J.B. & Cobb, C.W. (1989), *For the common good: Redirecting the economy toward community, the environment, and a sustainable future*, Beacon Press, Boston.

De Neve, N.JE., De Neve N.A., Christakis, J.H., Fowler B.S. Frey, G., (2012), Economics, and Happiness, CESIFO Working Paper No. 2946, Category 12: Empirical and Theoretical Methods, Original Version: February 2010, This Version August 2012

Diener, E. (1984) 'Subjective well-being' *Psychological Bulletin* 95: 3, pp. 542-575.

Diener, E. and Seligman, M., (2004), Beyond Money: Toward an Economy of Well-being, *Psychological Science in the Public Interest*, Vol 5., no. 1, pp. 1-31

Diener, E., Lucas, R.E. & Scollon, C.N. (2006), 'Beyond the hedonic treadmill: Revising the adaptation theory of well-being', *American Psychologist*, vol. 61, no. 4, pp. 305-14.

Dolan, P. (2014), Happiness by Design: Finding pleasure and purpose in everyday life, Penguin Random House, UK

Easterlin, R., A. (1974) 'Does economic growth improve the human lot? Some empirical evidence' In P.A. David and M.W. Reader (eds.) *Nations and households in economic growth; Essays in honour of Moses Abramovitz* (p. 89-125) New York: Academic Press

Easterlin, R.A., (1995) 'Will Raising the Income of all Increase the Happiness of All?' *Journal of Economic Behaviour and Organisation* 27: 1, pp. 35-47

Easterlin, R.A. (2005) 'Feeding the illusion of growth and happiness: A reply to Hagerty and Veenhoven, 2006, *Social Indicators Research* 74: 3, pp.429-443

Easterlin, R.A. (2003), 'Explaining happiness', *Proc Natl Acad Sci U S A*, vol. 100, no. 19, pp. 11176-83.

European Commission (2013), *Beyond GDP, Key quotes.* Retrieved on 02/07/2013 from http://www.beyond-gdp.eu/key_quotes.html.

Felber, C. (2010), *Die Gemeinwohl-Oekonomie, Das Wirtschaftsmodell der Zukunft*, Deuticke, Germany

Forrester, JW. (1971), World Dynamics. Wright-Allen Press, Cambridge.

Frank, R., 2011, *Darwin Economy: Liberty, competition and the Common Good*, Princeton University Press, USA

Frey, B.S. and Stutzer, A. (2001) *Happiness and Economics: How the Economy and Institutions affect Human Well-being*, Princeton University Press

Fürst, E., (2011), Ein Wegweiser in die Armut und ins Chaos, DiePresse.com, 30 January, viewed on 12 December 2014, http://diepresse.com/home/meinung/gastkommentar/629941/Ein-Wegweiser-in-die-Armut-und-ins-Chaos?from=suche.intern.portal

Graham, C. (2009), *Happiness around the world: the paradox of happy peasants and miserable millionaires*, New York: Oxford University Press

Gross National Happiness (GNH) Center (2013). Background of Gross National Happiness. Retrieved 02/07/2013 from http://www.gnhbhutan.org/about/The_background_of_Gross_National_Happiness.aspx

Hák, T., Janoušková S., Abdallah S., Seaford C. and Mahony S., (2012), Review report on Beyond GDP indicators: categorisation, intentions and impacts. Final version of BRAINPOoL deliverable 1.1, A collaborative project funded by the European Commission under the FP7 programme (Contract no. 283024). CUEC Prague, 18 October 2012

Hart, K., Laville J.L, Cattani, A. (eds) (2010), *The Human Economy: A Citizen's Guide* Cambridge: Polity Press

Haugh, H., (2005), 'A research agenda for social entrepreneurship', Social Enterprise Journal, Vol. 1 Iss 1 pp. 1 - 12

Headey B. (2006), Subjective Well-Being: Revisions to Dynamic Equilibrium Theory Using National Panel Data and Panel Regression Methods. *Social Indicators Research* 79: 369 – 403

Building Sustainable Legacies 5 *March 2015* © Greenleaf Publishing 2015

Helliwell, J., Layard, R., Sachs, J. (Eds.). (2012). *World Happiness Report 2012*. Sustainable Development Solutions Network: A Global Initiative for the United Nations. New York, USA

Jevons, W. S. (1866) Brief Account of a General Mathematical Theory of Political Economy, *Journal of the Royal Statistical Society*, London, XXIX (June 1866), pp. 282-87.

Kahneman, D. (2011), Thinking Fast and Slow, Penguin Books, London

Kahneman, D. and Deaton, A. (2010), High income improves evaluation of life but not emotional well-being, *PNAS*, Vol. 107, No.38, pp. 16489–16493

Kahneman, D., and Krueger, A. (2006) Developments in the Measurement of Subjective Well-Being *Journal of Economic Perspectives* 20: 1, pp. 3-24

Kemper, A., & Martin, R. L. (2010) After the fall: The global financial crisis as a test of corporate social responsibility theories. *European Management Review*, 7: 229-239.

Klimecki, O.M., Leiberg, S., Ricard, M. & Singer, T. (2014), 'Differential pattern of functional brain plasticity after compassion and empathy training', *Social Cognitive & Affective Neuroscience*, vol. 9, no. 6, pp. 873-9.

Korten, D. and Scharmer, O., (2014), Shaping a New Narrative for a New Economy, 8 December, viewed 3 December 2014, http://www.ceholmesconsulting.com/shaping-narrative-economy/

Kubiszewski, I., Costanza, R., Franco, C., Lawn, P., Talberth, J., Jackson, T., Aylmer, C., (2013). Beyond GDP: Measuring and achieving global genuine progress, *Ecological Economics* 93, pp. 57–68.

Kuznets, S. (1934). 'National Income, 1929–1932'. 73rd US Congress, 2d session, Senate document no. 124, page 7.

Leadbeater C. (1997) *The Rise of the Social Entrepreneur*. London: Demos.

Legatum Institute (2014). *The Legatum Prosperity Index*. Retrieved 29 November 2014, from http://www.prosperity.com/#!/

Leiberg, S., Klimecki, O. & Singer, T. (2011), 'Short-term compassion training increases prosocial behavior in a newly developed prosocial game', *PLoS One*, vol. 6, no. 3, p. e17798.

Layard, R. (2005) *Happiness: Lessons from a New Science* London Penguin

Lykken, D. and Tellegen, A. (1996), Happiness is a stochastic phenomenon. *Psychological Science* 7: 186-89

Martin, A., (2012), Happiness and Wellbeing, a New Economic Paradigm, The Global Policy debate and implications for multi-national businesses, MBA Research Dissertation, Exeter University, UK

McMahon, D., (2007), *The Pursuit of Happiness: A History from the Greeks to the Present* London: Allen Lane/Penguin

Max-Neef, M., (1995), Economic growth and quality of life: a threshold hypothesis. Ecological Economics 15 (2), 115–118.

Meadows, D.H. & Club of Rome. (1972), *The limits to growth; a report for the Club of Rome's project on the predicament of mankind*, Universe Books, New York.

Meadows D. (1999), *Leverage Points: Places to Intervene in a System*, The Sustainability Institute, VT USA

Meadows D. (2008), *Thinking in Systems*, In Wright, D. (Ed) Thinking in Systems, The Sustainability Institute, Chelsea Green Publishing, VT USA

Meadows, D. (2009). Leverage Points: Places to Intervene in a System. *Solutions*. Vol 1, No. 1. pp. 41-49. Retrieved on 21/05/13 from http://thesolutionsjournal.anu.edu.au/node/419

Miller, H., (2013), Patagonia founder takes aim: 'The elephant in the room is growth', *GreenBiz*, 1 March, viewed 12 December 2014, http://www.greenbiz.com/news/2013/03/01/patagonia-founder-takes-aim-elephant-room-growth

National Research Council. (2013). Subjective Well-Being: Measuring Happiness, Suffering, and Other Dimensions of Experience. Panel on Measuring Subjective Well-Being in a Policy-Relevant Framework. A.A. Stone and C. Mackie, Editors. Committee on National Statistics, Division of Behavioral and Social Sciences and Education. Washington, DC: The National Academies Press.

New Development Paradigm (NDP) Steering Committee and Secretariat, (2013), Happiness: Towards a New Development Paradigm, Report of the Royal Government of Bhutan

O'Donnell, G., Deaton, A., Durand, M., Halpern, D. and Layard, R (2014), Wellbeing and Policy—Report 2014, Legatum Institute, UK

OECD (2013), How's Life? 2013: Measuring Well-being, OECD Publishing, accessed at http://www.oecd-ilibrary.org/economics/how-s-life-2013_9789264201392-en viewed 15 January 2014

Office for National Statistics (ONS) (2014), Measuring National Well-being: Life in the UK, 2014 accessed at http://www.ons.gov.uk/ons/rel/wellbeing/measuring-national-well-being/life-in-the-uk--2014/art-mnwb--life-in-the-uk--2014.html on 8 April 2014

Pearce, D., Markandya, A., and Barbier E.B. (1989), Blueprint for a Green Economy, for the UK Department of Environment, Earthscan, UK

Pigou, A.C., Aslanbeigui, N. & Oakes, G. 2013, *The economics of welfare*, Fourth edition. Palgrave Macmillan, Houndmills, Basingstoke, Hampshire; New York.

Reynolds, P. D., Bygrave, W. D., Autio, E., Cox, L. W., & Hay, M. (2002). *Global entrepreneurship monitor*. Babson College, London Business School, Ewing Marion Kauffman Foundation.

Ricard, M. (2006), *Happiness: A guide to developing life's most important skill*, 1st English language edn, Little, Brown, New York

Ridley, M. (2003), *Nature via nurture: Genes, experience, and what makes us human*, 1st edn, HarperCollins, New York, N.Y

Rietveld, C., Cesarini, D., Benjamin D.J., Koellinger, P.D., De Neve J.E., Tiemeier, H., Johannesson, M., Magnusson, P.K.E, Pedersen, N.L, Krueger, R.F., and Bartels, M., (2013), Molecular genetics and subjective well-being, *PNAS*, June 11, vol. 110, no. 24, pp. 9692–9697

Roberts. D. & Woods, C. (2005). Changing the World on a Shoestring: The Concept of Social Entrepreneurship. *University of Auckland Business Review*, 45-51.

Building Sustainable Legacies 5 *March 2015* © Greenleaf Publishing 2015

Salvaris, M (2013), Measuring the Kind of Australia we want: The Australian National Development Index, the Gross Domestic Product and the Global Movement to Redefine Progress, *The Australian Economic Review*, Vol. 46, no. 1, pp 78-91

Seelos, C. & Mair, J. (2005). Social Entrepreneurship: Creating New Business Models to Serve the Poor. *Business Horizons*, 241-246.

Seidman, D., (2014), From Knowledge Economy to Human Economy, *Harvard Business Review*, accessed at https://hbr.org/2014/11/from-the-knowledge-economy-to-the-human-economy on 13 November 2014

Seligman, M. (2011) 'Building Resilience', *Harvard Business Review*, 89: 4, pp. 100-106

Stiglitz, J., (2009), Interview with Joseph Stiglitz in Pittsburgh 23 September 2009; min 1:30 http://youtube.com.

Sukhdev, P. (2012). *Corporation 2020: Transforming Business for Tomorrow's World*, Washington DC, USA: Island Press.

Ura, K., Alkire, S., Zangmo, T., Wangdi, K. (2012), A Short Guide to Gross National Happiness Index, Centre for Bhutan Studies, Thimphu, Royal Government of Bhutan

Veenhoven, R.R., and Hagerty, M.R. (2006) 'Rising Happiness in Nations 1946-2004' *Social Indicators Research* 79: 3, pp. 421-436

Veenhoven, R.R. (2012) 'Happiness and Well-being: Not quite the same' *Comments to the draft declaration 'Realizing the world we all want' Comments from participants on draft outcome document* http://www.2apr.gov.bt/index.php/background-reading/205 accessed 25th September 2013

Weber, J., & Marley, K. (2012). In search of stakeholder salience: Exploring corporate social and sustainability reports. *Business and Society*, 51 (4), 626-649.

Windsor, D (2012). Toward a General Theory of Responsibility and Irresponsibility. *2012 Proceedings of the International Association for Business and Society*, vol. 23, pages 48–59.

The Role of Business Law in the Jigsaw Puzzle of Sustainability

Beate Sjåfjell*

University of Oslo, Faculty of Law, Norway

This article presents the argument that reforming business law is a necessary contribution to the greening of our economies and societies. The article is specifically about European business law, while similar arguments can be made for other regions of the world.

Sustainable development has a strong legal position among the ultimate objectives of the European Union, underpinned by the growing recognition in the EU of the inextricable entity of humanity, our natural environment and our economic system. Contrary to common belief, EU law is not just about free movement and market integration. This article starts with the assertion that EU Treaty law contains the necessary elements for the EU to instigate change and take the lead to shift from the path of business as usual, towards a truly sustainable development. The codification of the sustainable development principle in the environmental integration rule in Article 11 TFEU is the key. Article 11 TFEU, properly interpreted, has significant legal implications for the institutions of the European Union, entailing direct obligations on all levels: Law-making, administration, supervision and judicial control.

This article thereafter shows the significance this has for the regulation of European companies and financial markets — central to the greening of our economies and societies — and how Article 11 TFEU should be implemented. A reform of European company law is central here, with a number of other areas of business law providing important contributions as well. The article concludes by presenting the core elements of work-in-progress reform proposals based *inter alia* on the results of the international Sustainable Companies Project.

- European Union Treaty law
- Sustainable companies
- Corporate social responsibility
- Directors' duties
- Purpose of the company
- Company law
- Planetary boundaries

* I would like to thank the international network of scholars of the Sustainable Companies Project and the participants at the Oslo workshop, where these reform ideas were hammered out, for insightful contributions — especially Jukka Mähönen, Filip Gregor, Mark Taylor and Georgina Tsagas. For encouragement and succinct advice during the whole process I am grateful to Chris Halburd, and for inspiring comments on a draft of this article, the wonderful editor Michael Townsend.

Beate Sjåfjell is Professor Dr. Juris at the University of Oslo, Faculty of Law. Beate is head of the Faculty's Research Group *Companies, Markets, Society and the Environment* (jus.uio.no/companies) and the international *Sustainable Companies* project (2010-2014), as well as of the new international project: *Sustainable Market Actors for Responsible Trade (SMART)*. Beate's publications include *Towards a Sustainable European Company Law* (Kluwer Law International, 2009), and the edited volumes *The Greening of European Business Under EU Law: Taking Article 11 TFEU Seriously* (Routledge, 2015, co-editor Anja Wiesbrock) and *Company Law and Sustainability: Legal Barriers and Opportunities* (Cambridge University Press, 2015, co-editor: Benjamin Richardson).

✉ University of Oslo, Faculty of Law, Department of Private Law, P.O. Box 6706 St Olavs plass, NO-0130, Oslo, Norway

💻 b.k.sjafjell@jus.uio.no

'Business as usual' is not an option

The discussion of whether we need a fundamental transition should be over. Ever stronger warnings from the Intergovernmental Panel on Climate Change emphasise that business as usual is a very certain path towards a very uncertain future, and that is just one of the planetary boundaries that we are transgressing or threatening. To secure a liveable and just society for ourselves, for our children and children's children, we need to find a new path towards a circular economy where social and economic development is ensured within the non-negotiable ecological limits of our planet. From this starting point, based on the knowledge that business as usual is not an option, the question is not whether but how we can achieve such a fundamental transition away from the push for infinite growth within finite resources and onto a path towards truly sustainable development. The topic for this article is the necessary contribution of business law in the jigsaw puzzle of sustainability. This article is specifically on European business law, while it is in its essence also relevant for other regions of the world.

Drawn by Katarina Sjåfjell, age 12

Sustainable development has a strong legal position among the ultimate objectives of the European Union (EU), underpinned by the growing recognition in the EU of the inextricable entity of humanity, our natural environment and our economic system[1] (Sjåfjell, 2009: 171-248). The Lisbon Treaty has further strengthened sustainable development as an overarching goal, in Europe and globally.[2] Contrary to common belief, EU law is not just about free movement and market integration, although in practice it may seem that way sometimes.[3] The lack of proper implementation of this overarching Treaty goal necessitates forward-looking legal scholarship, where we spell out what the Treaties require of EU law and policy.

This article builds on research-based insights that EU Treaty law contains the necessary elements for the EU to instigate change and take the lead to shift from the path of business as usual, towards a truly sustainable development. The codification of the sustainable development principle in the environmental integration rule in Article 11 of the Treaty on the Functioning of the European Union (TFEU) is the key. This codification has enhanced the position of sustainable development as an overarching objective and especially that of its environmental dimension (Nowaq, 2015).[4] Article 11 TFEU requires full integration of environmental protection requirements into all policies and activities of the EU with the aim of achieving sustainable development. Properly interpreted, Article 11 has significant legal implications for the institutions of the European Union, entailing direct obligations on all levels: law-making, administration, supervision and judicial control (Sjåfjell, 2015a).

In the next section this article discusses the significance this has for the regulation of European companies and financial markets, central to the greening of our economies and societies, and how Article 11 TFEU should be implemented in that area. A reform of European company law is the core here. The article concludes by presenting the core elements of work-in-

---

1   The ultimate objectives of the European Union are stated in the relevant provisions of the Treaties; until 1 Dec. 2009 particularly Article 2 of the former EC Treaty: the Treaty establishing the European Community (1957), last amended (and name changed to TFEU) by the Treaty of Lisbon, OJ 2008 C115 (consolidated version); as well as the former Art. 2 and Art. 6 of the Treaty on European Union (1992), last amended by the Treaty of Lisbon, OJ 2008 C115 (consolidated version), hereinafter referred to as the EU Treaty (abbreviated TEU in accordance with the new reference style of the Lisbon Treaty). Now see notably the new Art. 3 TEU.

2   Articles 3(3), 3(5) and 21(2)(d) and (f) TEU.

3   The withdrawal in December 2014 of the EU circular economy package is illustrative. This package could have been a first step towards a more sustainable economy and it is easy to understand the doubt as to whether this will be replaced by a 'more ambitious' package in 2015, see 'Recycling industry erupts as EU Commission ditches circular economy package', Ben Messenger, *Waste Management World*, 17 Dec. 2014 (online at www.waste-management-world.com/articles/2014/12/recycling-industry-erupts-as-eu-commission-ditches-circular-economy-package.html).

4   As discussed by Julian Nowaq, the wording of the provision was through the Maastricht Treaty changed from 'shall be a competent of' to 'must be integrated', laying down the foundations of the current justiciable version of what is now Article 11 TFEU.

progress reform proposals based *inter alia* on the results of the international Sustainable Companies Project.[5]

Reforming business law for sustainability

Business law is usually not included in the discourse on how to achieve sustainable development, not even in the discussion of the role of business in sustainable development. Business law in the EU today is first and foremost a vehicle of market integration, through the removal of obstacles and barriers, the facilitation and enabling of businesses and financial markets and the protection of shareholders and other participants, creditors and to a limited extent employees (Sjåfjell, 2009: 127-170). The argument for a new approach to business law in a sustainable development perspective may be summarised in three points: First, we are very far from achieving the goal of a sustainable development; second, we need the contribution of business to have any hopes of achieving the goal; and third, neither the voluntary contribution of business nor the current legal framework regulating the environmental impact of business is sufficient. A holistic reform is required.

Company law has a crucial role to play in the transformation towards sustainability because it provides the legal framework for the internal workings of the company, including its decision-making (Sjåfjell and Richardson, 2015). Based on the research of the Sustainable Companies Project,[6] company law has been identified as a crucial aspect of that which may be called the regulatory ecology of companies.[7] A thoughtful, well-founded reform of company law is therefore expected to impact on not only the decision-making within the company but also its relationship with its shareholders, its employees and society at large, by stimulating the enormous potential within business to create long-term, sustainable value through an internalisation of environmental and social externalities.

---

5 For more information about this University of Oslo-led project, see http://jus.uio.no/companies under Projects (last visited 22 Jun. 2014).

6 This project has had as its aim to integrate environmental concerns better into the decision-making in companies and has analysed the barriers and possibilities that company law, including the regulation (or lack thereof) of corporate groups, reporting requirements and accounting law, pose for the shift towards sustainable companies. Based on these results, reform proposals have been developed.

7 The use of 'regulatory ecology' in this company law and sustainability context is based on a presentation by Mark Taylor at the workshop 'Sustainable Companies in the EU', held at the University of Oslo 5-9 May 2014. This is more commonly discussed under the umbrella of 'polycentric regulation' (Black, 2008; Taylor, 2011).

This tentative reform proposal springs out of a research project that has had the deeper integration of environmental concerns into the decision-making of companies as its aim. Envisaged as the basis for a proposal for a new EU directive, and in recognition of the inextricable interconnectedness of environmental, social and economic aspects of business, this reform proposal encompasses all three dimensions (Sjåfjell, 2015b).

Article 11 TFEU entails that any legal basis in EU law is also a legal basis for protecting the environment, and shall be used as such if that is relevant as a contribution to sustainable development. This entails that as long as there is a legal basis for regulating a company law issue, there is also a legal basis for integrating environmental protection requirements in that company law legislation. The main idea of this tentative proposal would probably best be implemented through the adoption of a new company law directive, while changes in other directives may also be suggested.

While the mainstream corporate governance debate tends to regard maximisation of shareholder profit as the sole purpose of companies, this is, as a matter of law, to a great extent incorrect, especially understood as society's purpose with companies in aggregate (Sjåfjell et al., 2015).

No company law system insists on boards focusing only on returns for shareholders. In some jurisdictions environmental sustainability has begun tentatively to make inroads into the explicit duties of the board (Johnston, 2014; Lambooy, 2010). All jurisdictions expect boards to ensure environmental legal compliance. Generally company law across jurisdictions also allows boards to integrate environmental externalities beyond legal compliance, at least as far as the business case argument allows; i.e. as far as the case can be made that this is profitable for the company in the long run. Indeed, the cross-jurisdictional analysis of the Sustainable Companies Project has shown that there is a great unexplored potential in the current company law regimes for companies to shift away from the path of business as usual and onto a path towards sustainability by shifting their focus from short-term maximisation of returns to shareholders to long-term value creation (Sjåfjell et al., 2015).

However, boards do in aggregate not even choose the environmentally friendly, low-carbon option within the realm of the business case, let alone challenge the outer boundaries of the scope to pursue profit in a sustainable manner. This is evidenced through the cross-jurisdictional general lack of case law where board decisions are challenged on such grounds. This is because of the overriding social norm of shareholder primacy, which, supported by management remuneration incentives and other drivers, leads to an extremely narrow, short-term, profit maximisation focus (Sjåfjell et al., 2015). This has been pinpointed also by the EU Commission as a problem but not adequately acted on (Sjåfjell and Anker-Sørensen, 2013). The resulting practice of companies in aggregate is detrimental to those affected by climate change and environmental degradation today and to the possibility for future generations to fulfil their own needs. It is also damaging to any shareholder with more than a very short-term perspective on their investment, including institutional investors such as pension funds or sovereign wealth funds, as well as to the companies themselves.[8]

Shareholder primacy as the main barrier to sustainable companies has been allowed to flourish notably because the law has not specified what the societal purpose of companies is; leaving a vacuum that has been filled with this social norm (Sjåfjell et al., 2015). This also indicates a way forward. A reform that clearly spells out the societal purpose will set a key issue straight in a principle-based manner, enabling forward-looking sustainable business.

What urgently needs to be done is to clarify that while companies in the aggregate may and should have profit as their core purpose this should be achieved within the overarching societal purpose of sustainable development (Willard, 2014). The purpose of the company, as a matter of company law, needs to be redefined. To encourage the shift away from 'business as usual', it is necessary to internalise the fundamental recognition that there are ecological limits that we cannot transgress if we are to achieve sustainability. Long-term economic sustainability presupposes that business is conducted with respect for the ecological limits. If we are to achieve a safe operating space for humanity, we cannot continue with incremental improvements; neither can we focus on whichever environmental challenge gets the most attention at any given time. The concept of planetary boundaries (Rockström et al., 2009), state-of-the-art natural science, embodies this fundamental recognition and should form the space within which all economic and social development is to take place.

This concept should therefore be a key issue in a redefined purpose of companies as a matter of company law.[9]

---

8 While the preamble of the proposal for an amendment of the Shareholder Rights' Directive claims in Recital 2 that the financial crisis has 'revealed that shareholders in many cases supported managers' excessive short-term risk taking', an at least as valid concern is that shareholders have pressurised directors and managers to focus on short-term returns only.
9 The tentative reform proposal presented in a short form here was first proposed in a Nordic context early in 2014 (Sjåfjell and Mähönen, 2014) and further developed in an EU law context later the same year (Sjåfjell, 2015b).

Planetary boundaries

Source: Rockström *et al.* (2009a) and Steffen *et al.* (2011).[10]

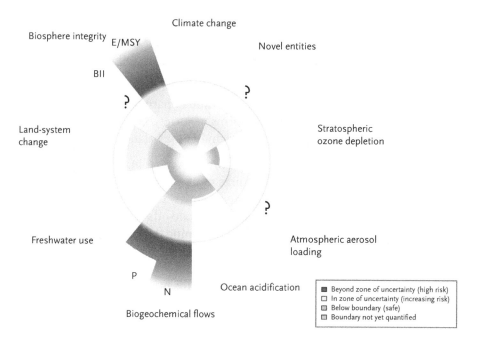

The redefined purpose of companies in an EU company law directive could for example be formulated like this: 'The purpose of a company is to create sustainable value within the planetary boundaries while respecting the interests of its investors and other involved parties'.

The most fundamental key issues here are the purpose of creating *sustainable value* and the space within with value can be created: *within the planetary boundaries*. A further development of this idea into a proper legislative proposal would require explanatory notes where the concept of *sustainable value* was given content. The basic idea is that *sustainable value* is long-term and inclusive, as opposed to short-term and exclusive pursuit of shareholder returns. Protection and promotion of the interest of the shareholders, other

---

10 The planetary boundaries include as shown in the figure above, biosphere integrity, global freshwater and land use, ocean acidification, atmospheric aerosol loading, stratospheric ozone depletion, cycling of phosphorus and nitrogen (biogeochemical flows) and novel entities (new substances, new forms of existing substances, and modified life forms that have the potential for unwanted geophysical and/or biological effects). It is estimated that humanity has already transgressed three of these boundaries: climate change, biosphere integrity, biogeochemical flows and land-system change (Steffen *et al.*, 2015). The planetary boundaries may be revised through new evidence, and scientific uncertainty is naturally unavoidable. The environmental precautionary principle is of essence. Indeed, the conceptual framework for planetary boundaries itself proposes a strongly precautionary approach, by 'setting the discrete boundary value at the lower and more conservative bound of the uncertainty range' (as stated already in Rockström *et al.*, 2009b).

investors and other involved parties, including employees, creditors and other contractual parties, is encompassed through the formulation that sustainable value is to be sought *while respecting the interest of its investors and other involved parties*.[11] Broader societal impact can also be included in *sustainable value* and *other involved parties* depending on how this is defined in explanatory notes and implemented, interpreted and put into practice.

Fitting comfortably into the teleological, dynamic EU law method, these concepts give room for development over time in pace with the development of generally accepted ethical norms of society, both in terms of which interests are included and of the balancing between them.

While the operationalisation of *planetary boundaries* in a company law and corporate governance context requires more work, the formulation *within the planetary boundaries* is used to signal clearly that these are indeed non-negotiable boundaries, where the room for trade-offs is limited. As a matter of principle there can be no trade-offs threatening the planetary boundaries, as opposed to balancing social and economic aspects, while recognising that the ultimate goal is to achieve not only a safe operating space for humanity but a safe and *just* space for humanity (Raworth, 2012).

We can envisage future development of sector guidelines and standards and merging natural science and corporate governance that to an even greater extent can allow a sector-by-sector and business-by-business definition of what staying within planetary boundaries entails. However, we can already now put forward a proposal on how to operationalise this purpose. The key components of such an operationalisation are to integrate the purpose into the duties of the board and require that each company draws up a long-term, life-cycle based business plan. The duties of the board are arguably the best place in the regulatory ecology of the companies to introduce the operational part of such a redefined purpose of the companies as this article proposes, because of the key role the board according to company law has in the governance of companies (Sjåfjell and Anker-Sørensen, 2013). This can be done by introducing the concept of *life-cycle based creation of sustainable value* as what the board is to promote and ensure. A life-cycle-based assessment is a key concept here, as a proper cradle-to-cradle assessment of the value creation of the company allows for a full overview of the environmental, social and economic consequences of the basis of the company's business (Ekern, 2015). This in turn allows for fundamental changes or slighter adjustments, as the case may be, of the business strategy of the company to ensure that that the value creation is indeed sustainable.

Realising the enormous potential for sustainable value creation within each company cannot be undertaken through regulation in a command-and-control, top-down manner. Rather, each company must identify its own

---

11 Using 'investors' rather than 'shareholders' recognises the complex structures of finance through debt, equity or grants.

individual, innovative way of creating sustainable value. To achieve this, and to ensure that it is brought right up to the level of the board, the duties of the board should encompass the drawing up of a long-term, life-cycle based *business plan*. Risk management and due diligence would be a part of the company's toolbox to ensure that the business plan is implemented within the company and its activities.

The business plan shall contain the long-term plan for the company.[12] The business plan shall describe how the company is to achieve life-cycle based value creation within the planetary boundaries, or more poetically, what is the company's long-term vision for sustainable value creation. A requirement for such a business plan, designed thoughtfully, would involve a standardisation of a process that companies wishing to achieve long-term sustainable value would need to do anyway. The standardisation would contribute to lowering costs and establishing a level playing field. As we will see below, this proposal presents a more structured and robust basis for the company's decision-making and its communication with its stakeholders than do the reporting requirements in many jurisdictions including the new EU requirements (Villiers and Mähönen, 2015).[13]

A life-cycle-based approach is key here, whereby this proposal fits well together with the integrated product policy of the EU where the life-cycle perspective is identified as the leading principle (Ekern, 2015). A life-cycle-based approach entails an assessment in a cradle-to-cradle perspective of a product, including every phase from the sourcing of the materials used in the production through the production, marketing and selling of the product, to the user phase and finally to the recycling or waste management of the product. This would enable the company to identify its potential for increased efficiency in use of energy and other resources and pinpoint and mitigate material negative environmental and social impacts. In the context of creating sustainable value within the planetary boundaries, the process would require identifying and mitigating material negative environmental and social impact. This may be possible to do through an adjustment of aspects of the life cycle of the business. However, it may also result in a decision to more fundamentally change the business strategy of the company. The purpose of sustainable value *within the planetary boundaries* requires transformation rather than incremental improvements of environmental and social performance. This would also mean that the companies that already have sustainable business models in the sense indicated here would gain the competitive advantage over companies that profit from environmental destruction and social inequality.

---

12 A tentative indication is that long-term here would be 15–30 years (or the full time span of the company, if it has a shorter time horizon).

13 Proposal for a Directive of the European Parliament and of the Council amending Council Directives 78/660/EEC and 83/349/EEC as regards disclosure of non-financial and diversity information by certain large companies and groups, COM(2013) 207 final – 2013/0110 (COD), adopted by the European Parliament April 2014.

A full life-cycle-based assessment to identify and mitigate negative environmental and social impacts, as described immediately above, would have to be undertaken for any products the company sells, either by the company itself, or by the manufacturer/supplier. This would be a way of dealing with the pulverisation of responsibility for environmental and social impacts that we see today through multinational groups of companies and international supply chains. Any European company would need to draw up its own life-cycle based business plan or substantiate that this was covered e.g. by a parent company's business plan. A life-cycle assessment would need to be conducted for any product involved in the value creation of a European company, either by the company itself or by the supplier.

An issue for further research will be how to ensure that such a reform is not circumvented through companies in third-world countries selling their products to European purchasers. Goods imported by or sold to European companies would already be covered by the tentative reform proposal indicated here. Among unresolved issues are direct sales to European consumers. Whether these are substantial enough issues to warrant additional regulation remains to be investigated.

The plan shall include milestones or objectives to be achieved along the way, and key performance indicators (KPIs) in as far as the impacts can be quantified, relevant to the specific plan of the company, which the company can report on annually. This should not mean that the company cannot in addition also set goals that are not (easily) quantifiable. The long-term plan should be broken down into shorter time segments,[14] entailing that the company at these regular intervals must undertake a full assessment of its business plan and consider necessary revisions.

The directors' duties could for example be formulated like this:

The board of the company is to ensure the life-cycle based creation of sustainable value. To this end, the board shall adopt and regularly revise a long-term business plan for the company, based on a life-cycle assessment of the company's main areas of business.

A mandatory table of contents of the business plan should be drawn up as an annex to the directive, to encourage proper compliance and comparability between companies. Giving the business plan a specific title could be considered, to ease reference to this requirement in other EU contexts. Guidelines endorsed by the European Commission should set out how the relevant and sufficient KPIs are to be selected according to the sector and concrete business plan of the company.

Effective enforcement of these duties is on the one hand necessary to ensure that the requirements become more than words on paper and that they are not used as a basis for greenwashing. A sensible starting point is to turn

---

14 For example, 15 years broken down into three or five year segments.

the drawing up of the business plan itself into an enforceable duty. This can easily be done for new companies by including it among the documents required to incorporate a new business. For existing companies, it can be required within a certain time-period, for example 18 months after the entry into force of the new rule. This could easily be enforced within the existing systems in the Member States by the company registrar, which could check the business plan for new companies (as it checks whether it has other relevant documents), and probably also for existing companies (as it checks whether accounts are sent in when they should), with the same type of sanctions as for other such core documents. With a minimum content of such a business plan, the registrar could then also check whether these items were filled in without evaluating the content.

The qualitative control of the business plan should probably be limited to the selection of KPIs to ensure that these core indicators against which the company is to report are relevant and sufficient. With guidelines or standards endorsed by the European Commission to identify the relevant and sufficient indicators, such a check, which only needs to be undertaken when the business plan is drawn up or fundamentally revised, should not be too burdensome to require. An issue to be developed further is how this could be undertaken; most likely it can be covered by auditors with experience with sustainability assurance.[15]

Obviously, implementing such a reform will have costs. On the other hand, there are also potential substantial benefits already in the short-term for the companies. The life-cycle assessment will have the added benefits of making legal compliance easier (because all aspects of production are brought onto the table); it will increase efficiency, cut costs, and allow for the identification and mitigation of environmental and social impacts. Done properly, it would involve a full internalisation of environmental and social externalities, allowing the company to create value in a truly sustainable manner. Instigating such a transition within companies would also reduce the need for detailed external regulation. It would further stimulate the innovation that we need to encourage the achievement of the dual goal of Europe having the market leaders of tomorrow and of business being part of the transformation from the highly risky 'business as usual' towards sustainability.[16]

The proposal here would give a clear duty on which to report and give content to the recently adopted non-financial reporting requirement on the EU level.[17]

---

15 See e.g. the Sustainability Accounting Standards Board www.sasb.org accessed 21 June 2014

16 This could e.g. lead to innovative business models such as renting a service of having a product instead of selling the product, and could contribute to mitigating the incompatibility of the goals of the EU's Europe 2020 strategy of (infinite) growth and a 'smart, sustainable and inclusive economy', http://ec.europa.eu/europe2020/ (accessed 10 July 2014).

17 See n. 13 above and Villiers and Mähönen, 2015.

In the directive this is to be done on a comply-or-explain basis. As a part of the tentative reform proposal presented here, this reporting should be an obligatory part of the management report, linked directly to the business plan idea presented above, and reporting against the key performance indicators approved as a part of that plan.

The company would in other words be required to report annually, in its management report, on the milestones and key performance indicators (KPIs) identified in the business plan; i.e. on how the company meets its objectives and how the impacts are measured. This would make best practice mandatory. The content of this could be further developed in guidelines, a first step of which is on its way through the guidelines the Commission is to develop according to the new non-financial reporting directive (Villiers and Mähönen, 2015).

This would be the second point of enforcement of the proposed reform: the reporting against the KPIs. The accuracy of the information provided in reports should ideally be verified, which could be envisaged on the basis of sector guidelines or standards endorsed by the European Commission.

An issue for further development is how the reporting should be verified. Is a consistency check by auditors sufficient, or should one envisage a full sustainability assurance?[18] These requirements could be tightened through subsequent reform, but ideally a full sustainability assurance requirement should be in place from the beginning.

To make such a reform effective, the key concept of creating sustainable value within the planetary boundaries would also need to be included in other areas of business law. This can for example be done by giving the business plan requirement legal significance in financial market law, public procurement, state aid and consumer regulation (Sjåfjell, 2015b; Wiesbrock, 2015).

Transformation rather than incremental improvement is necessary. Truly transformative proposals are bound to meet resistance. This does not mean that they are not politically possible to achieve a sufficient majority on. There are a number of signs indicating that we are living in a time where conventional wisdom is questioned, and where sustainability issues are discussed in contexts where such topics were previously ignored. With shareholder primacy increasingly being denoted as the 'world's dumbest idea' (Welch in Stout, 2012), there are indications that management thinkers as well as some of the largest companies in the world are moving beyond the detrimental goal of short-term maximisation of returns to shareholders (Serafeim, 2013; Christensen and van Bever, 2014).

---

18 See e.g. the Sustainability Accounting Standards Board www.sasb.org accessed 21 June 2014.

This article presents an idea for a reform of company law that, if enacted, could form one of the pieces of the jigsaw puzzle of sustainability that we so urgently need to get into place.

Bibliography

Black, J. (2008) 'Constructing and Contesting Legitimacy and Accountability in Polycentric Regulatory Regimes,' *Regulation and Governance 2.*

Christensen, C. M. and van Bever, D. (2014) 'The Capitalist's Dilemma', Harvard Business Review, Jun. 2014, 60-68.

Ekern, E. M. (2015) 'Towards an Integrated Product Regulatory Framework Based on Life Cycle Thinking', in Sjåfjell, B. and Wiesbrock, A. (eds) *The Greening of European Business under EU Law: Taking Article 11 TFEU Seriously*, London: Routledge, 144-162.

Johnston, A. (2014) 'Reforming English Company Law to Promote Sustainable Companies', in *European Company Law*, 11(2), 63-66.

Lambooy, T. (2010) *Corporate Social Responsibility: legal and semi-legal frameworks supporting CSR: developments 2000–2010 and case studies*, Deventer: Kluwer.

Nowaq, J. (2015) 'The Sky is the Limit: on the drafting of Article 11 TFEU's integration obligation and its intended reach', in Sjåfjell, B. and Wiesbrock, A. (eds) *The Greening of European Business under EU Law: Taking Article 11 TFEU Seriously*, London: Routledge, 15-30.

Raworth, K. (2012) 'A safe and just space for humanity: can we live within the doughnut', (Online), Available: www.oxfam.org/sites/www.oxfam.org/files/dp-a-safe-and-just-space-for-humanity-130212-en.pdf (Oxford: Oxfam International), (last visited 2 Jan. 2014).

Rockström, J. et al (2009a) 'Planetary boundaries: exploring the safe operating space for humanity', (Online), Available: www.ecologyandsociety.org/vol14/iss2/art32/ (last visited 14 Jan. 2014).

Rockström, J. et al (2009b) 'Supplementary Information', (Online), Available: www.stockholmresilience.org/ (under research; planetary boundaries), (last visited 20 Dec. 2013).

Serafeim, G. (2013) 'The Role of the Corporation in Society: An Alternative View and Opportunities for Future Research', Harvard Business School Working Paper 14-110. Available: SSRN: ssrn.com/abstract=2270579 (last visited 21 Jun. 2014).

Sjåfjell, B. (2009) *Towards a Sustainable European Company Law*, Alphen aan den Rijn: Kluwer Law International.

Sjåfjell, B. (2015a) 'The Legal Significance of Article 11 TFEU for EU Institutions and Member States', in Sjåfjell, B. and Wiesbrock, A. (eds) *The Greening of European Business under EU Law: Taking Article 11 TFEU Seriously*, London: Routledge, 51-72, and also available on SSRN: ssrn.com/abstract=2530006.

Sjåfjell, B. (2015b) 'Corporate Governance for Sustainability: The Necessary Reform of EU Company Law', in Sjåfjell, B. and Wiesbrock, A. (eds) *The Greening of European Business under EU Law: Taking Article 11 TFEU Seriously*, London: Routledge, 97-117.

Sjåfjell, B. and Anker-Sørensen, L. (2013) 'Directors' Duties and Corporate Social Responsibility (CSR)', in Birkmose, H. S., Neville, M. and Sørensen, K. E. (eds), *Boards of Directors in European Companies*, Alphen aan den Rijn: Wolters Kluwer.

Sjåfjell, B. and Mähönen, J. (2014) 'Upgrading the Nordic Corporate Governance Model for Sustainable Companies', *European Company Law* (2014) 11, 58–62

Sjåfjell, B. et al (2015) 'Shareholder Primacy: the Main Barrier to Sustainable Companies' in Sjåfjell, B. and Richardson, B. (eds), *Company Law and Sustainability*, Cambridge: Cambridge University Press (forthcoming 2015).

Steffen, W., et al (2015) 'Planetary boundaries: Guiding human development on a changing planet' (Online), *Science*, Vol 347, No 6223, Available: DOI: 10.1126/science.1259855 (last visited 10 Mar. 2015).

Taylor, M. B. (2011) 'The Ruggie Framework: Polycentric Regulation and the Implications for Corporate Social Responsibility,' Etikk i Praksis, Nordic Journal of Applied Ethics 5, no. 1.

Villiers, C. and Mähönen, J. (2015) 'Article 11: Integrated Reporting or Non-Financial Reporting?', in *The Greening of European Business under EU Law: Taking Article 11 TFEU Seriously*, Beate Sjåfjell and Anja Wiesbrock (eds), London: Routledge, 118-143.

Welch, J. in Stout, L. (2012) *The Shareholder Value Myth*, San Francisco: Berret-Koehlers Publishing.

Wiesbrock, A. (2015) 'Sustainable State Aid: A full environmental integration into EU state aid rules?', in Sjåfjell, B. and Wiesbrock, A. (ed.) *The Greening of European Business under EU Law: Taking Article 11 TFEU Seriously*, London: Routledge, 75-96.

Willard, B. (2014) 'Better is Not Good Enough: Toward True Corporate Sustainability', (Online), Available: www.greattransition.org/document/better-is-not-good-enough-toward-true-corporate-sustainability (last visited 21 Jun. 2014).

Exploring a One Planet Mindset and its Relevance in a Transition to a Sustainable Economy

Sally Jeanrenaud, Inmaculada Adarves-Yorno and Nicolas Forsans

Business School, University of Exeter, UK

Exeter's One Planet MBA (OP MBA), co-founded and delivered with WWF International, is helping develop a new generation of business leaders, integrating sustainability thinking across its business education curriculum, and fostering a "One Planet Mindset". But what is a One Planet Mindset? And what is its significance in a transition to a sustainable economy? This paper draws on the sustainability and management literature, and explorations with students to offer some preliminary reflections on these questions. It makes the case that a One Planet Mindset aggregates knowledge, values and skills which help deliver positive outcomes for people, planet and prosperity. It engages a new metaphor of nature as a living planet – one that recognizes that the health of the economy is rooted in, and not independent of, living planetary systems. Such a mindset provides a powerful lever for transforming, self, business and society in the contested transition to a sustainable economy.

- One Planet MBA
- Mindsets
- Values
- Business
- Sustainable Economy
- Transition

Dr **Sally Jeanrenaud** is a Senior Research Fellow in Sustainable Development, Business School, University of Exeter. She has over twenty years experience in international sustainable development, with research, policy, management and field experience from Asia, Africa and Western Europe. Her research interests lie in areas of the transitions to sustainable economy, sustainability-oriented innovation, innovations inspired by nature, and in multi-stakeholder and collaborative approaches. Sally teaches the 'Changing Business Environment' and the 'Biomimicry and Business' modules on the One Planet MBA, and also supervises PhD, and post graduate dissertations.

✉ Business School
Streatham Court
Rennes Drive
Exeter, UK EX4 4PU

🖥 s.jeanrenaud@exeter.ac.uk

Dr **Inmaculada Adarves-Yorno** is a Senior Lecturer in Leadership, working at the University of Exeter. She has a five-year degree in Psychology, two masters and a PhD in social and organizational psychology. She has received awards and fellowships from the Spanish Ministry of Social Issues, Spanish Ministry of Culture, the British Council, the Economic and Social Research Council and Exeter University. As a leadership developer she has designed, led and collaborated in a wide range of programmes (residential, undergraduate, Masters, MBAs, including the One Planet MBA). She is specialised in experiential learning, authentic leadership, change agency and personal development.

✉ Business School
Streatham Court
Rennes Drive
Exeter, UK EX4 4PU

🖥 I.Adarves-Yorno@exeter.ac.uk

Prof **Nicolas Forsans** is a professor in International Strategic Management, with expertise in the fields of international business and corporate strategy, and in the disruption of business models by emerging technologies (digital in particular). His research publications have focused on multinational firm strategies, the rising importance of emerging economies in global business and the foreign direct investment activities (mostly through mergers and acquisitions) of emerging country multinational firms in the western world.

✉ Business School
Streatham Court
Rennes Drive
Exeter, UK EX4 4PU

🖥 N.Forsans@exeter.ac.uk

Progress is impossible without change, and those that cannot change their minds, cannot change anything (George Bernard Shaw).

Objectives and questions

The objective of this paper is to explore the idea of a One Planet Mindset and its significance in a transition to a sustainable economy.

We ask two main questions:

▶ What is a One Planet Mindset?

▶ Why is it significant in a transition to a sustainable economy?

To help answer these question we briefly review the One Planet concept as framed by WWF; some of the literature on mindsets and sustainable business; and draw on research with MBA students.

Background

A One Planet perspective

WWF, the world's leading conservation NGO, has developed several 'One Planet' initiatives over the last 13 years. The inspiration for and scientific underpinnings of its One Planet approach are derived from WWF's Living Planet Report, one of the world's leading science-based analyses on the health of the planet, which has been published every two years since 1998.

worldwide we need 1.5 planets to regenerate the natural resources we currently use

These indicate that worldwide we need 1.5 planets to regenerate the natural resources we currently use: for example, we are harvesting more fish than the oceans can replenish and emitting more carbon into the atmosphere than the forests and oceans can absorb. However, WWF claims that it is not too late to change course, and that we do have the capacity to create a prosperous future that provides food, water and energy for the 9–10 billion people who are expected to share the planet in 2050, but only if all stakeholders—governments, companies, communities, citizens—step up to this challenge (WWF 2012).

WWF's work draws on and is corroborated by a wealth of other evidence-based analyses on the state of the planet, including the work of the Global Footprint Network; the Zoological Society of London; UNEP's Global Environmental Outlook (GEO) reports; the Stockholm Resilience Centre and its research on planetary boundaries (Rockstrom *et al.* 2010) among others. While WWF has a particular expertise in framing the environmental sustainability challenges, other organisations spell out the global social and economic risks more explicitly.

The World Economic Forum, for example, put 'income disparity' and 'unemployment and underemployment' in their top five global risks to the economy in their 2014 Global Risks Register. Oxfam (2013) reports that 1% of the population owns almost half the world's wealth. Seven out of ten people live in countries where economic inequality has increased in the last 30 years. They claim that the growing divide between the haves and have-nots is unethical, socially divisive, politically corrosive, ecologically damaging, and actually damages economic growth in the long term.

In relation to economic challenges, Korten (2010) claims that our current economic system is unstable and driving boom and bust cycles, creating debt and holding governments hostage to financiers. He asserts that we have created a financial sector that favours speculation and 'phantom wealth' over real investment. Sukhdev (2012) also points out our subsidy and fiscal regimes support 'business-as-usual'. Some US$1 trillion per annum are spent on perverse subsidies which support the old fossil-fuel based, throw-away economy, and thwart efforts to build a new sustainable one.

> **our economy is unsustainable, unfair, unstable and is making us unhappy**

Stuart Wallis (2011) succinctly sums it up as '4 U's': our economy is **unsustainable**, **unfair**, **unstable** and is making us **unhappy**; and we need a transition to an economy which is socially just and maximises wellbeing within environmental limits.

WWF's 'One Planet Perspective' (2012:106) articulates five key policy dimensions and priority action points intended to inform better choices for a living planet: 1) preserve natural capital; 2) produce better; 3) consume more wisely; 4) redirect financial flows; and 5) govern resources equitably. Its One Planet Perspective underpins a range of solution-oriented One Planet initiatives that have been developed over the last 13 years (see Appendix 1). These have several features in common:

> **WWF's 'One Planet Perspective' articulates five key policy dimensions and priority action points intended to inform better choices for a living planet**

▷ The idea that we only have one planet's worth of resources to provide for a rapidly growing population

▷ A critique of the existing economic system which relies on fossil fuels, and on unsustainable take-make-waste production and consumption systems

▷ Positive solutions, through its One Planet initiatives, which offer inspiring ideas about how to create more sustainable futures

▷ A perspective that addresses the interdependent environmental, social and economic dimensions of sustainability challenges

Illustration: Klaus Elle

> Management decisions that support ecosystem integrity and pro-poor growth and development

> The idea that sustainability challenges can be transformed into commercial opportunities and that business and industry can be a positive force for good

> The need to work with multiple stakeholders including governments, business and communities to co-create solutions at a system-level

> An underlying narrative that as living beings, we are dependent on a 'living planet', and that the health of the planet is fundamental to the economy

WWF's framing of a One Planet Perspective provides an important basis for our discussion of One Planet Mindsets within the context of the One Planet MBA. But we are also interested in how the programme and students are co-creating a One Planet Mindset as the MBA adapts and evolves over time.

The significance of mindsets

What is a mindset, and why are we interested in them in the context of developing sustainable businesses and the transition (albeit contested) to a sustainable economy?

Illustration: Klaus Elle

People define mindsets in various ways. For example, Meadows (1999) describes mindsets as the shared ideas in the mind of society; the deepest set of beliefs about how the world works, or shared social agreements about the nature of reality. Mindsets give rise to systems which structure our societies and economies. Mindsets such as 'one can own land' or 'nature is a stock of resources to be converted to human purposes', or 'growth is good' may be taken for granted by some societies, but may completely dumbfound others. Korten (2014) describes similar elements as 'stories' and argues that human beings live by shared cultural stories: 'They are the lens through which we view reality. They shape what we most value as a society and the institutions by which we structure power.'

> **Meadows describes mindsets as the shared ideas in the mind of society; the deepest set of beliefs about how the world works**

Meadows (1999:18) claims that change agents who have managed to intervene in a system at the level of mindsets or paradigms have hit a leverage point that totally transforms those systems. (The concepts of mindset and paradigm are used interchangeably in Meadows' 1999 paper.) Changing mindsets is considered more powerful than changing other things in a system such as rules, incentives or infrastructures. Mindsets are often considered harder to change than anything else in the system, and their role is therefore ignored or undervalued. Society tends to resist

> **change agents who have managed to intervene in a system at the level of mindsets or paradigms have hit a leverage point that totally transforms those systems**

challenges to its paradigms harder than it resists anything else; but in a single individual changes can happen in a split second: 'a falling of scales from the eyes, a new way of seeing' (Meadows 1999:18).

> our current economic and business mindsets are based on outdated paradigms of economic thought

To so many thought leaders and writers, our current economic and business mindsets are based on outdated paradigms of economic thought; and these are driving us towards social, environmental and economic collapse (Korten, 2001; Bakan, 2003; Porritt, 2007; Haque 2011). There are a growing number of initiatives helping to define what a new sustainable economy might look like, and how governments, businesses and communities need to work together for systems change (Jackson, 2009; Generation, 2012; Elkington, 2012; Mackey and Sisodia, 2013; Scharmer & Kaufer, 2013; Townsend and Zarnett, 2013). Acknowledging the work of many pioneering leaders, Townsend and Zarnett (2013) have developed an initial synthesis of nine design principles underpinning a sustainable economy:

1. Less growth, more wellbeing

2. A broader view of what capital means

3. Based on responsible enterprise, adding real value, where it is needed

4. Holistic systems thinking; aligned with the circular economy

5. Enabled by a well-functioning money system

6. Away from speculative bubbles, towards creating longer-term real wealth

7. Shared ownership and distribution of resources and wealth

8. Based on collaboration and striving together

9. Founded on new institutions and greater systemic resilience

A transition to a sustainable economy has risks and opportunities for business. Among other things we need to reform markets to address real needs of all stakeholders; reduce waste and costs, and create new jobs; reform company reporting; redesign incentive structures to encourage long-term behaviour; create new forms of share and ownership structures; and redirect investments. Additionally, Scharmer & Kaufer (2013) argue that we need to transform ourselves as part of this process, to make a shift from ego-system to eco-system economies. This involves 'changing the inner place from which we operate' in order to transcend old mindsets and open up to new ones.

Managerial mindsets

How can a new generation of business leaders open up to new possibilities and learn to manage themselves, their organisations and relationships in the context of transition to a sustainable economy?

While Gosling and Mintzberg (2003) do not locate their work within the context of a shift to a sustainable economy, we argue that their work on managerial mindsets is relevant to managing such a transition. They claim that Five Managerial Mindsets need to be integrated in effective management practices. This integration evolves from weaving together reflection on action in various domains, relating to self, organisations, contexts, relationships and change. These might be considered as 'attitudes' which open up space for new possibilities to emerge.

> **Five Managerial Mindsets need to be integrated in effective management practices**

▷ **Reflective mind-set: managing self**. This emphasises developing meaning from reflection on one's own experiences as a manager. Reflection might be considered the 'suspended space' between where the manager has had an experience and the explanation for it, where an individual is able to make connections, including possible future options. Organisations need people who are capable of seeing beyond their own personal behaviour or immediate situations, and see the world around them

▷ **Analytical mind-set: managing organisations**. Organisations are complex systems of people, physical assets, techniques, and structures and which require an analytic mindset and approach to solving problems. But managing organisations going beyond the superficialities of data and analysis, to understanding the deeper meanings of structures and systems. Complex decision-making involves more than dealing with quantitative data; it requires understanding qualitative (soft) data and the nuances underlying them, such as values

▷ **Worldly mind-set: managing context**. An important distinction is made between the words 'globalisation' and 'worldly'. The former involves perceiving the world from a distance, while the latter delves into the cultures, habits and customs of peoples living near and far. Effective organisations manage to create both a global and worldly view within their operations, while less successful ones tend to reflect the cultures of the home office managers. Developing 'worldly' perspective involves responding to specific conditions.

▷ **Collaborative mind-set: managing relationships**. This involves understanding and managing the relationships between people, rather than managing the people themselves. A collaborative mindset entails transcending the 'heroic' style of leadership, and the conventional belief that managers must bestow their 'blessing' upon their staff. Rather it is 'leadership in the background', building commitment among people through engagement with them, and encouraging dispersed forms of leadership

▷ **Action mind-set: managing change**. Many managerial skills are needed to move an organisation in a new direction, and to maintain its course. It involves coordinating the aspirations and energies of others and encouraging them towards a common vision; and understanding the landscape in which people are working and collaborating. Managers must know which things need to be changed and which ones must be maintained. Carefully planned action and reflection are both required and need to be integrated

Graham-Rowe (2011) reflects whether good business skills and sustainability skills are increasingly the same thing, and says that it is not entirely clear how sustainability skills differ from the skills you would expect any competent business leader to possess. Perks (cited in Graham-Rowe 2011), however, argues that: 'Sustainability adds context. You can be a good leader but if you don't have a view of where the world is heading then you won't have the skills to make your business succeed.'

Transition to a sustainable economy

What kinds of knowledge, values and sustainability skills are required by a new generation of business leaders in building sustainable businesses and making a transition to a sustainable economy? The literature in this area is vast, and we can only touch on a few key points.

Knowledge

John Elkington (1999), in his book *Cannibals with Forks*, was one of the first thinkers to bring concepts of sustainability into business management, by defining the significance of 'the triple bottom line' to business. This emphasises social, environmental and economic dimensions of corporate performance, instead of an exclusive focus on the financial bottom line. These are also sometimes described as the three Ps: People, Planet and Profit; or the 3 Es: Equity, Ecology and Economy, and have become an influential concept in business thinking and practice.

> Triple bottom line thinking implies that business leaders require new types of knowledge and ways of thinking to be effective

Triple bottom line thinking implies that business leaders require new types of knowledge and ways of thinking to be effective. UNEP (2013) points out that sustainability challenges have significant implications for reorienting strategy, leadership, governance, supply chains, operations, financing, reporting and reputation, as resources become scarcer, prices increase, and government regulations get stricter. Adams *et al.* (2012) explore how sustainability is driving innovation in business, across products, processes, organisations, and systems; while Volans (2013) outlines how business is creating breakthrough solutions in tackling the world's greatest environmental, social and governance challenges, and shaping new forms of capitalism.

These all suggest that a new generation of business leaders will require a much broader knowledge of the role of business in society, of the interlinked sustainability challenges and how to transform these into business opportunities. It will require a shift from silo to systems thinking, and an ability to link knowledge from different domains. For example, they will require a knowledge of living planetary systems and their boundaries, such as the carbon, water and nitrogen cycles, and how business operations interact with them (Whiteman *et al.* 2012); ways to value the contribution of natural capital (UNEP 2011); and knowledge about social challenges and how to create healthy, vibrant communities (Strandberg 2014). They require familiarity with innovative business models which are transforming how corporations operate, such as the circular economy (Ellen MacArthur Foundation 2011), the sharing economy (Botsman and Rogers 2010), and the green economy (UNEP 2011), and how to create shared value propositions (Porter and Kramer 2011).

Values

In his book, *The Sustainable Self*, Paul Murray (2011) highlights the critical role of the 'personal' dimensions of sustainability as well as the 'professional' ones. He puts personal motivations, values, attitudes and beliefs centre-stage and emphasises the relationship between personal core values and sustainability values, and how these influence our potential to deliver change.

Murray's work draws on deeper psychological understandings of values. Schwartz (1992), for example, defines a value as: 'a desirable trans-situational goal varying in importance, which serves as a guiding principle in the life of a person or other social entity' (p. 21). In their theory of universal content and structure of values Schwartz and Bilski (1990) identified value orientations. These are defined as clusters of compatible values or value types. Research has found a relationship between certain value orientations and pro-environmental attitudes and behaviour (Hansla *et al.* 2008) as well as corporate social responsibility (CSR) (Potocan & Nedelko, 2014). For example, self-transcendence values ('valuing and caring for all people and nature') have been found to be positively related to pro-environmental and CSR attitudes and behaviour, whereas self-enhancing values (concerned with power and achievement) have been shown to be negatively related to pro-environmental and CSR attitudes and behaviour.

> we are also interested in the role of personal values, and how these motivate behaviour

In our framing of One Planet Mindsets, then, we are also interested in the role of personal values, and how these motivate behaviour. These represent an important sensibility towards nature and people that is not captured by technical knowledge alone.

Skills

Graham-Rowe (2011) claims that the task of ensuring that business leaders have the skills they need to take their companies forwards into a new economy is one of the most pressing challenges that businesses are likely to face over the next five years.

However, the Institute of Environmental Management and Assessment (IEMA) (2014) report that many organisations are 'asleep at the wheel' when it comes to developing the skills and capabilities needed to address sustainability challenges, which would enable them to survive and stay competitive. For example, 82% of organisations surveyed by IEMA say that their procurement staff are not capable of contributing to their environmental and sustainability agendas. Asda recently launched its resilience plan after research revealed that an estimated 95% of all the fresh produce on its shelves is at risk from climate change.

> Leaders and managers need skills-training in how to integrate sustainability into long-term decision making, throughout their organisations and value chains

Leaders and managers need skills-training in how to integrate sustainability into long-term decision making, throughout their organisations and value chains. Skills-training is also required to help businesses adapt manufacturing processes and service delivery to cope with supply volatility and to work towards a 'circular economy' (IEMA 2014). Business in the Community (2010) outline leadership skills such as the ability to develop long-term vision, to inspire, empower, collaborate, innovate, and communicate; while other research highlights the skills needed to embed sustainability within organisational cultures (Bertels, 2010); and collaborative partnerships to unlock a new wave of innovation for sustainability (Gray and Stites, 2013).

IEMA (2011) has developed a skills map which identifies the types of knowledge, analytical thinking, communications, sustainable practices, and leadership for change required by business in a transition to a sustainable economy, relevant to actors fulfilling different roles in organisations. They claim that employing people with the right skills, knowledge and expertise could save UK businesses £55 billion a year, through energy and resource savings.

Towards a One Planet Mindset

This paper explores how One Planet Mindsets are developed and articulated in the context of the One Planet MBA, in the Business School, University of Exeter, United Kingdom. (For more information on the origins and description of the OP MBA see Appendix 2.)

As described on its website, the One Planet MBA was founded in collaboration with WWF International in 2011, and aims to develop a new generation of business leaders equipped with the knowledge, skills and understanding required to create, build and develop sustainable, profitable businesses capable of succeeding in a fast changing international business landscape. It recognises that environmental, social and financial changes are challenging traditional business models, and that tomorrow's business leaders across the globe must recognise and embrace these challenges and be capable of developing more sustainable business practices and processes.

As a preliminary exploration of the One Planet Mindset among One Planet MBA students we looked at two things:

▶ The knowledge that they independently seek to generate and develop during their dissertations. This will indicate that on top of the material delivered to them, students actively seek to generate knowledge relevant to building sustainable businesses and the transition to a sustainable economy

▶ Whether their self-transcendence values overcompensate for their self-enhancement values. As noted above, self-transcendence values are strongly related with pro-environmental and pro-social behaviours and indicate sensibilities associated with sustainability values

Knowledge

We reviewed the titles and objectives of 117 dissertation and consultancy reports researched by full-time and executive students between 2011 and 2014. We tracked the use of the word sustainability in the titles or objectives, and the use of at least two of the three dimensions of sustainability (environmental, social or economic) in their work. Dissertation titles reflect topics of interest to the students while consultancy projects are largely framed by corporate partners, with some input from students.

A review of 117 dissertation and consultancy projects undertaken by One Planet MBA students between 2011 and 2014 indicate that 59% of their independent projects addressed a sustainability theme explicitly.

> A review of 117 dissertation and consultancy projects undertaken by One Planet MBA students between 2011 and 2014 indicate that 59% of their independent projects addressed a sustainability theme explicitly

Original and groundbreaking work has been undertaken on subjects such as: happiness and wellbeing and new business metrics; the circular economy; stakeholder engagement; shared value; materiality analyses; sustainable supply chain analyses; servisation (shifting from delivering products to delivering services); sustainable finance; youth leadership for sustainability; net positive impact; sustainable tourism; sustainable soil management; sustainable marketing and communications; food waste; waste management; business models which scale sustainable practices; biomimicry for business; renewable energies; green economy; sustainability and human resources; storytelling and sustainability, among many others. The dissertations and reports undertaken by One Planet MBA students suggest that they are generating knowledge relevant to a transition to a sustainable economy.

Values

To explore the value orientations of the OP MBA students we draw on both quantitative and class discussions.

In the quantitative research we were interested to explore whether OP MBAs have higher self-transcendent values than self-enhancement values. The sample was composed of 24 students, and the data was collected 8 weeks after they started the programme. We used a short version of the Schwartz (1994) value scale.

the value orientations of OP MBA students would support the pro-environmental and pro-social attitudes and behaviours

Results show how self-transcendent values ($M = 8.98$, $SD = 1.60$) were significantly higher than self-enhancement values ($M = 7.54$, $SD = 1.62$), $t (24) = 2.75$, $p = 0.01$. These results suggest that the value orientations of OP MBA students would support the pro-environmental and pro-social attitudes and behaviours.

Informal but structured class discussions on the values, knowledge and skills required for a transition to a sustainable economy have also been a feature of modules taught in the OP MBA as well several delivered on the MBA in Responsible Management in Audencia School of Management in Nantes, France. Discussions have been held with international cohorts of 30–40 students in both locations. Several sets of class contributions were recorded, and incorporated in Table 1.

Framing a One Planet Mindset

Combining knowledge from the literature, research and explorations with students we offer a preliminary framework for understanding the features of a One Planet Mindset. We present values, knowledge and skills against the triple bottom line of People, Planet and Prosperity. We have replaced the original framing of 'P for Profit' with 'P for Prosperity', to reflect evolving ideas of wealth and wellbeing, which do not preclude financial profit, but have a more nuanced understanding of what constitutes prosperity (Jackson 2009).

We present values, knowledge and skills against the triple bottom line of People, Planet and Prosperity

Table 1 Framing a One Planet Mindset

	Planet	People	Prosperity
Values	Respect for all life	Social justice	Profit, Wealth, Wellbeing
Knowledge of challenges & new models	**Challenges:** e.g. Carbon Biodiversity Water Resources Waste Planetary-boundaries	**Challenges:** e.g. Population & consumption Equality & rights Work conditions Access	**Challenges:** e.g. Unsustainable growth Externalities Fiscal regimes Subsidies
	New Models: e.g. Circular economy	**New Models:** e.g. Sharing economy	**New Models:** e.g. Green economy
Personal and professional skills	Relatedness to nature Long term vision Global & local perspectives Systems thinking 'Smart' data & analytical skills	Authentic leadership Listening Inspiring change Global and worldly Relationship skills Influencing skills Collaborative Stakeholder management	Commercial Awareness Integrity Responsibility Sustainability-oriented innovation (SOI) New business models New funding models Triple bottom line accounting skills

Conclusion: building a sustainable legacy

In conclusion we will reflect on the two questions posed at the beginning of the paper, and offer a few thoughts on further research.

What is a One Planet Mindset?

We propose that the One Planet Mindset can be understood as a new 'umbrella' concept, or leitmotif; one that aggregates the reflective managerial mindsets already developed with the specific knowledge, value orientations and skills required for a transition to a sustainable economy. We have suggested a preliminary framework that integrates values, knowledge and skills with the sustainability issues of people, planet and prosperity. As Bogue remarked in 1994: 'We need leaders with concepts in their heads, convictions in their hearts and caring in their hands'.

In relation to **values**, preliminary research suggests that the One Planet Mindset appeals to change agents with intrinsic and self-transcendent values (sensibility towards life, nature and people) which motivate pro-environmental and pro-social attitudes and behaviours. In relation to **knowledge**, we argue that a One Planet Mindset implies a critique of many of the assumptions of the existing economic system, and supports the development of innovative business and economic models with positive impacts for planet, people and prosperity, through new articulations of leadership, strategy, operations, capital, finance, governance, and metrics. In relation to **skills** and behaviours, a One Planet Mindset prioritises attributes required for transforming self, business and society (e.g. ethical, long-term vision, holistic, collaborative, globally minded, innovative, reflective, etc.).

Why is it significant in a transition to a sustainable economy?

> **When mindsets shift we see and value new things and behave in different ways**

Following Meadows (1999) we maintain that mindsets embed our deepest beliefs and assumptions about the world and frame what is considered worthy and valuable. Although mindsets are invisible and intangible, they influence our attitudes, values, knowledge and behaviours, which shape our societies and economies. When mindsets shift we see and value new things and behave in different ways. The focus on fostering new mindsets highlights a powerful lever of systems change. It also draws attention to some of the inner dimensions of social change in the transition, critical to a sustainable economy.

So far we have argued that a One Planet Mindset addresses and integrates the kind of knowledge, values and skills required by a new generation of business leaders to guide a transition to a sustainable economy which implies different goals, values, models, skills, power structures and measures of success. But, perhaps a more profound answer to the question of why a One Planet Mindset is significant in a transition to a sustainable economy is

> **A One Planet Mindset thus represents a new sensibility towards nature. It re-connects us and re-grounds us in a living planet**

that it engages a new metaphor of nature: not nature as a machine, or set of resources (that business is increasingly worried about in a complex and 'resource-constrained' world), but as something alive, as a set of inter-connected and self-organising planetary systems— with limits.

As living beings we are dependent on these life-supporting systems for the air we breathe, the water we drink and the soil we grow our crops in. The health of the economy is rooted in, and not independent of them. A One Planet Mindset thus represents a new sensibility towards nature. It re-connects us and re-grounds us in a living planet. It recognises that while we cannot change the laws of nature, we can learn to live within nature's budget, and work with the grain of life. This, we propose, contributes a potentially powerful and transformative new mindset through which to do business and build a sustainable economy.

Future research

The ideas presented in this paper prompt further questions, such as the role of educational programmes in supporting and fostering such mindsets among a new generation of business leaders; the challenges of taking a sustainable business and economy agenda forward; and the relevance of working on the inner dimensions of social change.

Our observations suggest that educational programmes, such as Exeter's One Planet MBA, have important roles to play in helping develop such mindsets. They do this by integrating sustainability across the curricula, rather than treating it as a bolt on module; developing innovative pedagogies which promote experiential learning, opportunities for personal reflection and collective reflection and transformation; and by encouraging multicultural and multi-stakeholder engagement. But we need to learn more about how such programmes are transformed and delivered, and their impacts on students to understand how they foster new ways of thinking and acting.

In this paper we have also mentioned the idea of a 'contested' transition to a sustainable economy. There are clearly challenges in developing new mindsets, and in taking a sustainable economy agenda forward. Society clings to ideologies and resists changing mindsets more strongly than anything else. New business and economic models profoundly challenge existing belief systems, power structures, and vested economic interests. We need to understand the transition through a political lens, as much as through economic, technical or social ones, and much more research on the politics of the transition is required.

The focus on mindsets also helps underline the importance of the inner dimensions of social change, and the role of personal transformation as part of the transition process. Meadows (1999:19) talks about a further and even more powerful lever of systems change, which is the capacity to transcend mindsets altogether, if only for a moment, 'to let go into not knowing' and 'to open up the spacious possibility of choosing new mindsets'. It is in this space of mastery over mindsets that people throw off addictions and bring down empires and have impacts that last for millennia. Understanding the role of mindfulness practices will be another fertile area of research in understanding the transformation of self, business and society.

References

Adams, R., Jeanrenaud, S., Bessant, J., Overy, P., Denyer, D. (2012): *Innovating for Sustainability: A Systematic Review of the Knowledge*. NBS, Canada.

Bakan, J. (2003): *The Corporation. A Documentary*

Bertels, S., Papania, L., and Papania, D. (2010): *Embedding Sustainability in Organizational Culture. A Systematic Review of the Body of Knowledge*. Canada: Network for Business Sustainability (NBS).

Bogue, E. G. (1994). *Leadership by Design: Strengthening Integrity in Higher Education*. Jossey-Bass Higher and Adult Education Series. Jossey-Bass Inc., San Francisco, CA.

Botsman, R. & Rogers, R. (2010): *What's Mine is Yours. The Rise of Collaborative Consumption*. New York: Harper Collins.

Business in the Community (2010): *Leadership Skills for a Sustainable Economy*. http://www.bitc.org.uk/our-resources/report/leadership-skills-sustainable-economy (accessed 4/1/15).

Elkington, J. (1999): *Cannibals with Forks. The Triple Bottom Line of 21st Century Business*. Oxford: Capstone.

Elkington, J. (2012): *Zeronauts: Breaking the Sustainability Barrier*. London: Routledge.

Ellen MacArthur Foundation (2011): *Towards the Circular Economy. Economic and business rationale for an accelerated transition*. Ellen Macarthur Foundation.

Generation (2012): *Sustainable Capitalism*. London: Generation Investment Management LLP. https://www.generationim.com/media/pdf-generation-sustainable-capitalism-v1.pdf (accessed 4/1/15).

Gosling, J. and Mintzerberg (2003): The Five Minds of a Manager. *Harvard Business Review*.

Graham-Rowe, D. (2011): Sustainability skills and good business skills are increasingly the same thing. *Guardian Sustainable Business Blog*. http://www.theguardian.com/sustainable-business/blog/sustainability-skills-business-skills-same (Accessed 4/1/15).

Gray, B. & Stites, J. (2013): *Sustainability through Partnerships. Capitalizing on Collaboration. A Systematic Review of the Body of Knowledge*. Canada: Network for Business Sustainability (NBS).

Hansla, A., Gamble, A., Juliusson, A., Gärling, T. (2008). The relationships between awareness of consequences, environmental concern, and value orientations. *Journal of Environmental Psychology, 28*, 1-9.

Haque, U. (2011): *New Capitalist Manifesto. Building a Disruptively Better Business*, Harvard Business Press.

IEMA (2011): *Skills Map* http://www.iema.net/skills (accessed 4/1/15).

IEMA (2014): *Preparing for the Perfect Storm. Skills for a Sustainable Economy*. Institute for Environmental Management and Assessment.

Jackson, T. (2009): *Prosperity without Growth. Economics for a Finite Planet*. London: Earthscan.

Korten, D.C (2001): *When Corporations Rule the World*. USA: Kumarian Press, and Berrett-Koehler.

Korten, D.C. (2010): *Agenda for a New Economy. From Phantom Wealth to Real Wealth.* Berrett-Koehler Publishers, Inc. San Francisco.

Korten, D.C. (forthcoming 2015): *Change the Story, Change the Future. A Living Economy for a Living Earth.* A Report to the Club of Rome. Oakland, CA: Berrett-Koehler Publishers.

Mackey, J. and Sisodia, R. (2013): *Conscious Capitalism: Liberating the Heroic Spirit of Business.* Harvard Business School Publishing Corporation.

Meadows, D. (1999): *Leverage Points. Places to Intervene in a System.* The Sustainability Institute.

Murray, A. (2011): *The Sustainable Self.* London: Earthscan.

Porritt, J. (2007): *Capitalism as if the World Matters.* Oxon: Earthscan.

Porter, M. & Kramer, P. (2011): Creating Shared Value. *Harvard Business Review.* January - February 2011.

Potocan, V. and Nedelko, Z. (2014), A New Socio-economic Order: Evidence About Employees' Values' Influence on Corporate Social Responsibility. *Syst. Res.* doi: 10.1002/sres.2264.

Oxfam (2013): The cost of inequality: how wealth and income extremes hurt us all. *Oxfam Media Briefing.* Ref 02/13 http://www.oxfam.org/sites/www.oxfam.org/files/cost-of-inequality-oxfam-mb180113.pdf (accessed 4/1/15).

Rockström, J., Steffen, W., Noone, K., Persson, A., Chapin, F. S., Lambin, E., Lenton, T., Scheffer, M., Folke, C., Schellnhuber, H.J., Nykvist, B., de Wit, C.A., Hughes, T., van der Leeuw, S., Rodhe, H., Sörlin, S., Snyder, P.K., Costanza, R., Svedin, U., Falkenmark, M., Karlberg, L., Corell, R.W., Fabry, V.J., Hansen, J., Walker, B., Liverman, D., Richardson, K., Crutzen. P., Foley, J.A. (2010): A Safe Operating Space for Humanity. *Nature* **461**, 472-475.

Scharmer, O. and Kaufer, K. (2013): *Leading from the Emerging Future. From Ego-System to Eco-System Economies. Applying Theory U to Transforming Business, Society and Self.* San Francisco: Berrett-Koehler Publishers.

Schwartz, S. H. (1992). Universals in the content and structure of values: Theoretical advances and empirical tests in 20 countries. In M. Zanna (Ed.), *Advances in experimental social psychology*, Vol. 25 (pp. 1–65). Orlando, FL: Academic Press.

Schwartz, S. H. (1994). Are there universal aspects in the structure and contents of human values? *Journals of Social Issues*, 50(4), 19–45.

Schwartz, S. H.,Wolfgang, B. (1990) Toward a theory of the universal content and structure of values: Extensions and cross-cultural replications. *Journal of Personality and Social Psychology, 58,* 878-891.

Strandberg, C. (2014): *Social Value Business Guide.* http://corostrandberg.com/wp-content/uploads/2014/09/business-guide-to-social-value-creation-2014.pdf (accessed 4/1/15).

Sukhdev, P. (2012): *Corporation 2020. Transforming Business for Tomorrow's World.* Washington DC: Island Press.

Townsend, M. & Zarnett, B. (2013): *A Journey in Search of Capitalism 2.0.*

Earthshine & Toronto Sustainability Speaker Series. http://www.earthshinesolutions.com/docs/A-Journey-in-Search-of-CAP2_Clean-Slate_Oct_2013.pdf (accessed 16/1/15).

Volans, (2013): *Breakthrough. Business Leaders, Market Revolutions.* London: Volans.

Wallis, S. (2011): The Four Horsemen of Economics. YaleGlobal Online http://yaleglobal.yale.edu/content/four-horsemen-economics (accessed 4/1/15).

Whiteman, G., Walker, B., Perego, P. (2013): Planetary Boundaries: Ecological Foundations for Corporate Sustainability. *Journal of Management Studies.* 50, 307-336.

World Economic Forum (2014): *Global Risks 2014.* Ninth Edition. Insight Report. http://www3.weforum.org/docs/WEF_GlobalRisks_Report_2014.pdf (accessed 4/1/15).

WWF (2012): *Living Planet Report 2012. Biodiversity, biocapacity and better choices.* Gland, Switzerland: WWF International.

WWF (2014): *Living Planet Report 2014. Species and Spaces, People and Places.* Gland, Switzerland: WWF International

UNEP (2010): *Towards a Green Economy. Pathways to Sustainable Development and Poverty Eradication.* Nairobi, Kenya: United Nations Environment Programme.

UNEP (2013): *GEO-5 for Business. Impacts of a Changing Environment on the Corporate Sector.* United Nations Environment Programme.

Appendix 1: the One Planet brand

Working with business, governments, communities and other organisations, WWF has developed a number of solutions-oriented (and trademarked) One Planet initiatives since 2002 to address the sustainability challenges. Amongst others these include:

▷ **2002 One Planet Living**. Founded with BioRegional which provides ten One Planet Living Principles to create easy, attractive, affordable lifestyles for an average person to live sustainably

▷ **2007 One Planet Leaders**. A training course run jointly with IMD in Switzerland from 2010, designed to inspire and equip leaders to drive change and build businesses that reduce footprint and create value for people and planet

▷ **2007 One Planet Business**. A system-change network with multiple stakeholders to develop workable solutions to issues such as mobility, food, housing, recognising that business can be a major driver in helping to shape a sustainable global economy

▷ **2007 One Planet Food**. Aims to reduce the global environmental and social impacts of food production and consumption, and works with business and governments

▷ **2009 One Planet Economy**. A two-year EU FP7 funded project focused on developing a footprint family of indicators (ecological, carbon and water) to track the demands of human consumption on the planet

▷ **2010 One Planet MBA**. Run jointly with the Business School, University of Exeter, UK aims to embed sustainability across the entire MBA curriculum

WWF (2012: 106) has outlined a 'One Planet Perspective' which highlights five key dimensions and 16 priority policy actions aimed to increase positive environmental, social and economic benefits:

1. **Preserve natural capital**. Significantly expand protected areas; halt the loss of priority habitats, restore damaged ecosystems

2. **Produce better**. Reduce inputs and waste in production systems; manage resources sustainably, scale-up renewable energy production

3. **Consume more wisely**. Change energy consumption patterns; promote healthy consumption patterns; achieve low-footprint lifestyles

4. **Redirect financial flows**. Value nature; account for environmental and social costs; support and reward conservation, sustainable resource management and innovation

5. **Govern resources equitably**. Share available resources; make fair and ecologically informed choices; measure success beyond GDP; sustainable population

Appendix 2: short history on the origins of the One Planet MBA

Aims

The aim of the OP MBA is to develop a new generation of business leaders equipped with the knowledge, skills and understanding required to create, build and develop sustainable, profitable businesses capable of succeeding in a fast changing international business landscape. It recognises that environmental, social and financial changes are challenging traditional business models, and that tomorrow's business leaders across the globe must recognise and embrace these challenges and be capable of developing more sustainable business practices and processes.

One of the informing ideas of the OP MBA is that sustainability is mainstreamed into every MBA subject area, rather than treated as a separate or 'bolt on' sustainability module. Sustainability is understood to embrace environmental, social and economic challenges (rather than being considered a 'green' topic), and to provide a context, which stimulates innovative and smart business models and solutions. Thus (to varying degrees) the sustainability thread runs through and provides context for all its core and elective modules: strategy, leadership, economics, innovation, supply chain, operations, marketing, financing, and reporting, etc. It is also a programme that supports participants seeking personal transformation and systemic transformation.

History

The Business School, University of Exeter and WWF International have a five year partnership to deliver the One Planet MBA (2011–2016), giving the University of Exeter the exclusive right to use the One Planet MBA brand within the UK during this time. The original concept note for the One Planet MBA was developed in 2009, and the development of the programme commenced in 2010 with an innovation cohort.

The history of the One Planet MBA is rooted in WWF's former One Planet Leaders (OPL) programme, which offered a five-day training course for business executives, which ran between 2007 and 2013 in Switzerland (and run in collaboration with IMD from 2010). This programme aimed to inspire and enable managers to innovate at strategic and operational levels based on an understanding of sustainability issues. It, in turn, evolved out of WWF's bespoke in-house training programmes with companies such as Nokia, who continued to provide support to the wider international initiative.

By the end of 2009 WWF's OPL programme had already graduated over 100 participants from companies such as Nokia, Canon, Lloyds TSB, Unilever and Shell among others. It had also already developed an association with the Business School and initially with the Department of Geography at the University of Exeter, which provided speakers on the course, and accreditation for its OPL programme. By that time WWF was learning that it was successfully engaging and inspiring leaders to change practices within their companies. Companies were sending people onto the programme on a regular basis demonstrating their satisfaction with the course; and the alumni were becoming an enthusiastic and active lobby group for change both within and outside their organisations.

However, WWF also recognised that its OPL format made it hard to reach large numbers of business leaders, and to cover every relevant business subject. It thus developed ambitions to scale up the impact of this initiative, and steps were taken in 2009 to develop a flagship One Planet MBA with the Business School, University of Exeter to attempt to influence a radical transformation of MBA curricula.

The title One Planet MBA was specifically chosen to make a statement, and to make explicit a fundamental assumption that we only have one planet's worth of resources to provide for over 7 billion people. Increasing resource scarcities and growing social inequalities made it imperative that business people were educated in a manner that was different from the past. It was seen as an opportunity to leverage the relationship with WWF International and its business partners, to develop a distinctive and innovative educational model that helped transform educational paradigms, priorities and pedagogies.

In 2011 co-founder Jean-Paul Jeanrenaud from WWF International (2011) said:

> Most MBAs are really geared towards training future leaders who will measure business success in terms of profitability and maximizing shareholder value. The One Planet MBA is attempting to change this business culture from the inside out; not by teaching different skills about how to run a business, but more through a shift in mindset. It starts from the standpoint and recognition that business-as-usual is neither desirable nor feasible long-term. Money per se is not evil, but it has to be directed to serve the wider good of humanity and the planet.

Transforming the programme

A strategic decision was made to reform Exeter's former MBA programme, rather than add an additional OP MBA. The module descriptors and module handbooks for each module of the MBA were reviewed, new learning outcomes added, new materials and reading lists developed. The MBA was launched in 2010 with a co-innovation year after several months of relationship building, staff recruitment and curriculum development.

The Dean of the Business School continues to be important champion of the new programme at the start of the process, and supported its progress with the School, and University. A new Director of the One Planet MBA was recruited at the outset, to manage the transition from the old to new programme, including managing relationships with existing faculty. The OP MBA is delivered in collaboration with WWF International, and WWF staff teach on several of its modules, which brings credibility to the programme on environmental and many business innovation issues. It is apparent that the transformation of an existing programme requires a core group of faculty who 'buy into' the changes and who help support it politically within the School.

The development of the OP MBA has required some new staff recruitment, and often involves bringing in specialists to help support the teaching of subjects, with a knowledge of sustainability issues. Many existing faculty have been willing to adapt their materials and approaches, and have also learned 'on the job', by selecting new case materials, undertaking new research projects, setting sustainability-oriented assignments for the students.

Partnerships with business

The Business School and WWF have both had a long history of working with business which has generated a wealth of knowledge and associations with the corporate sector. WWF has been instrumental in founding international sustainability market initiatives such as the Forest Stewardship Council (FSC), Marine Stewardship Council (MSC) and the Roundtable on Responsible Palm Oil (RSPO) with over 1,600 business and other partners. It has worked on many transformational and challenge partnerships over the years, with Lafarge, Nokia, Coca Cola, Unilever, IKEA, etc. It is involved in working with companies to reduce CO_2 emissions and toxic pollution, to conserve biodiversity, transform supply chains, operations, and purchasing decisions, and to govern resources better. The partnership with WWF also gives the Business School access to companies in China working on climate change initiatives through the WWF Climate Savers Network.

The OP MBA has developed relationships with 10 sponsorship companies: Coca Cola Enterprises, IBM, Lafarge, Thomson Reuters, Nokia, Canon, The

Co-Operative Group, IKEA, Lloyds Bank Group, and Atos. Several of these corporate connections developed out of the WWF challenge partnerships, and represent some of the most progressive businesses who see sustainability as a means of value creation and competitive advantage. The partnerships are leveraged to provide conceptual materials, speakers, and cases studies on innovative and pioneering approaches in business.

Challenges

There are several challenges in creating a One Planet MBA in the context of a transition to a sustainable economy. While it is highly valued as innovative and distinctive, the programme is competing in a commoditised and hyper competitive market, dominated by league tables which privilege traditional criteria of success. Thus, a major challenge for the One Planet MBA lies in creating a differentiated offering that increases it market appeal to students and recruiters alike. Partnerships between organisations in co-designing and co-delivering innovative programmes are potentially creative and powerful, but not always easy to manage, because of different values, culture, models and metrics of success. They demand collaborative skills and competencies, and regular review of goals, objectives and roles to avoid slipping into traditional models of service delivery.

Awards

The OP MBA has won a number of awards since 2012:

▷ 2013: Ranked in the top three worldwide, and first in the UK by Corporate Knights

▷ 2012: Ranked in the top 50 worldwide by the Washington-based Aspen Institute

▷ 2012: Winner, AMBA Innovation award

▷ 2012: Best new programme, Green Gown Awards

For more information on the One Planet MBA see: http://business-school. exeter.ac.uk/opmba/.

A 2x2 to Change the World

Jill Bamburg

Pinchot University, USA

The author has over 20 years' of experience teaching management to mid-career adults. In this article, she shares a framework she has developed to help her students think about how they might want to use their business skills to make a positive impact in the world. The framework is a 2x2 matrix, built around two dimensions of a world-view. One axis distinguishes between those who believe a "'win-win' world is possible" and those who believe a "'win-lose' world is inevitable." The other axis tests attitudes toward the existing political economic order, one viewing the current economic system as satisfactory, the other viewing an alternative economic system as required. The 2x2 yields four quadrants: replicate, reform, replace and retreat. The author offers a number of examples of successful approaches to building a better world for each quadrant. She concludes that "it's all good work" and encourages students to determine their own best path based on personality and passion.

- MBA students
- Vocation
- Change the world
- Worldviews
- Economic system
- Economic alternatives

Jill Bamburg is the President of Pinchot University, one of the pioneering Sustainable MBA programs in the US. She is also the author of *Getting to Scale: Growing Your Business without Selling Out* (Berrett-Koehler, 2006). She is a parent, a rower, a reader, a lover of art and music, and a baby boomer beginning to think about life after work. Her passion is working with adult students and helping them to become effective change agents, whose professional work is totally aligned with their personal values.

✉ President, Pinchot University, Suite 400, 220 S. Second Ave., Seattle, WA 98110 USA

🖥 jill.bamburg@pinchot.edu

One of the most valuable tools I acquired in business school was the 2x2 matrix.

With it, I was able to transcend the dreary black and white world of either/or choices and move into the heady realm of two-dimensional space, the four-quadrant world. And despite the 2x2's continuing appearance of reductionism, by casting the x and y axes as continuums, I was able to paint with enough shades of grey to satisfy my desire to illuminate business problems.

I actually went further than that, and began using 2x2s to gain insight into other kinds of problems. To offer one example from the realm of menu planning, I could place the presence or absence of gluten on the x-axis and the presence or absence of dairy on the y-axis, and develop a dinner menu capable of addressing the dietary preferences of most (albeit not all) of my dinner guests. At one point, I even developed a 2x2 party game where the audience throws out random topics for each axis, and the contestants (in most cases, I ran unopposed) put together amusing labels and stories to cover each of the quadrants.

For the last 12 years or so, I've been refining and presenting a 2x2 matrix with a more serious purpose: the challenge of helping my MBA students figure out what they want to be when they grow up or, to use Mary Oliver's better formulation, what it is they 'plan to do with [their] one wild and precious life'.

A word about context: my MBA students are not typical MBA students. For starters, they're already grown up. They come to us as adult learners, ranging in age from 22 to 68, with a median age of 32. Second, and far more important, they've already decided against the narrow vision of a traditional business career dedicated to the proposition of maximising shareholder value. They come to us already committed to building careers as change agents with business their chosen vehicle for social change.

But they come to us divided on an essential question: should they try to change the system from within—or should they pursue a more radical path? Evolution or revolution? Incremental change or transformation? 'Which is best?' they want to know. Which will be most effective—and which will be a waste of time?

My answer is always the same: 'It's all good work'.

By which I mean it is all work that needs to be done and we cannot know, in advance, which approach will succeed in the end. Therefore, it is critical that we, collectively, pursue both paths, according to our talents, temperament and current placement within the larger system. By recognising that 'it's all good work', I have tried to reduce the amount of time spent in this particular debate in order to spend more on the more important debate, the battle with the mainstream over whether change is needed at all.

Illustration: Klaus Elle

Enter the 2x2

To get to the next level of discussion with my students, I offer them the following 2x2, one step at a time.

The vertical axis first:

Win–win world is
possible

Win–lose world is
inevitable

Technically, we don't know whether a 'win–win world is possible'—we have never seen such a thing—which leads directly to the opposite conclusion, that a 'win–lose world'—the only world we have ever known—is 'inevitable'. Although the truth of either proposition is unknowable, the consequences of each belief are profound, as the matrix ultimately makes clear.

Horizontal axis next:

Current system   Alternative system
  = the solution   = required

By the 'current system', I essentially mean the combination of capitalism and democracy that Frances Fukiyama famously called 'the end of history'. Ironically, he and other defenders of the status quo would be at the far left of the diagram, while the campers of the Occupy Wall Street movement would be at the far right.

When we put the two axes together, we have the 2x2 frame for the emerging quadrants (Fig. 1).

Figure 1 The complete 2x2 matrix.

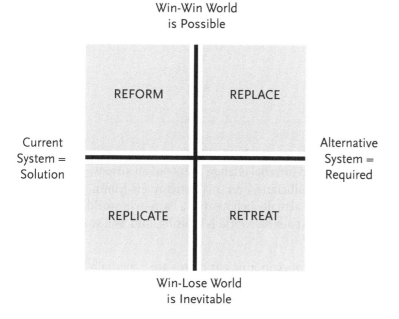

Replicate

In discussing the matrix, I always begin with the bottom left quadrant, the world as we know it. I believe that many of the people in this quadrant would self-identify as conservatives. They believe that the current capitalism system is the best economic structure the world has been able to devise to date, and that the solution to the problem of winners and losers is to work on creating more winners. Thus, the goal of those who choose to work in this quadrant is to replicate the current system to extend its reach and make its benefits available to more people.

More liberal practitioners may beg off on the ultimate merits of capitalism, but still argue for the practicality, immediacy and importance of ending the poverty of individuals, families and communities. Workers in this quadrant place a lot of emphasis on entrepreneurship—particularly microenterprise and microcredit—as vehicles for extending the benefits of capitalism to those who have been excluded from previous waves of prosperity. Traditional notions of community economic development—bringing Big Business back into communities abandoned by the last generation of Big Business—also fall into this quadrant.

There are many people and organisations doing good work in this quadrant. A few that come to mind: Mohammad Yunus and the Grameen Bank, Paul Polack and International Development Enterprises (IDE), the Skoll Foundation and its work in social enterprise, even version 2.0 of the Base of the Pyramid efforts. They may have a larger transformational agenda, but they tend to work through market mechanisms to create more winners, one individual, one enterprise, one community at a time.

Reform

Moving up one quadrant is the land of Reform, where we find corporate CSR professionals and internal change agents of all stripes, government regulators and liberal politicians, even mainstream environmental groups. Whether these individuals actually believe that a 'win–win world is possible', they certainly believe that a *better* world is possible and well worth working towards.

They assume that our current economic structures are essentially benign, just in need of reform.

About half of my students fall into this category—although many question their choice after the first quarter of our core curriculum, which calls into question many of the fundamental tenets of capitalism. Those who pursue this path point with justifiable pride to the scale of the impact of relatively small decisions—millions of tonnes of solid waste diverted from landfills, millions of tonnes of CO_2 not sent into the air, millions of gigawatts of energy avoided, billions of gallons of water saved in their plants.

When waste is the enemy, the profit-maximising interests of shareholders are aligned with the conservation values of environmentalists. Thus, the concept of 'eco-efficiency' is a pretty easy sell—assuming that the timelines for the payoffs can be equally well aligned (a very big assumption in today's short-term-focused financial markets). In all cases, the reform agenda relies upon making the 'business case' for change within the context of the current system.

In many cases, advocates of the reform agenda have focused on reporting, with the Global Reporting Initiative (GRI), CDP (formerly the Carbon Disclosure Project), the International Financial Reporting Standards (IFRS) and the Sustainability Accounting Standards Board (SASB) being four prominent examples. With KPMG reporting that 93% of the world's 250 largest companies currently file corporate responsibility reports, the battle over the necessity or desirability of reporting is over—the battle has now shifted to the standards that can be used to evaluate performance.

Replace

This is the quadrant for revolutionaries and idealists—those who believe that the dominant economic paradigm is the problem and can imagine alternatives that might work better. In many cases, these alternatives are local, small scale, grassroots experiments. Some add up to grand notions like the sharing economy or the creation of a local food economy as a substitute for industrial agriculture. Others are designed to stay small and local, achieving scale through replication based on example and inspiration.

About half of my students fall into this category, many of them betting that the current system will collapse within their lifetime and wanting to be in position with on-the-ground alternatives when the collapse occurs. The smaller scale of their revolutionary vision sometimes strikes me as inadequate to the challenge before us—until I remember the wholesale destruction wrought by the larger social experiments of the 20th century. Small is not only beautiful, it is considerably less dangerous.

Within this quadrant are experiments with local currencies, co-housing, regional food hubs, bike share systems, community tool libraries, and a host of other on-the-ground alternatives to the institutions of the dominant economic system. Many others use digital technology as substitutes for, or enhancements of, more traditional ways of doing things. The new businesses built around the Internet of Things hold the promise of enabling us to move from the uniformity and waste of mass production into a world of smaller scale, locally produced and more customised offerings. Some require significant capital investment, reinforcing the capitalist tendency toward concentration of wealth and resources; many others do not, potentially supporting a more egalitarian arrangement.

Retreat

This quadrant is a permanent home for some, a temporary haven for many more. Who among us has not sometimes wished to bury his or her head in the sand and just get away from it all? This is the quadrant of both solace and despair.

Here the belief is that greed and selfishness, winners and losers, dominance and subordination are inevitable aspects of the human condition that have now been firmly—and forever—embodied in our economic and political institutions. There is no hope for change at the systemic level; there are only individual lives that are either more or less satisfying. Those who opt to Retreat are committed to taking care of themselves and their families in an increasingly hostile world.

For some, this is the quadrant of the spirit, a place of transcendence and renewal, a way of jumping off the economic treadmill and into the deeper questions of existence. I find increasing numbers of students talking about the necessity of a transformation of consciousness as the only way out of our current dilemma. First enlightenment, then the laundry, as the Buddhists would have it.

In reality, very few of us—myself and my students included—occupy only one of these quadrants. Most of us bounce around a bit. Some of us, quite a bit.

The quadrants have been useful in helping students to frame their commitment to social change in terms of their own unique personalities, and in some cases, in terms of their life journeys. Some have the belief that the virtues of capitalism outweigh the vices and seek to extend the benefits of free enterprise to those whose previous opportunities have been limited. Some have the stomach for fighting the system from within. Some have the risk profile for creating new things. And some are tired of fighting and seek a place of refuge far from the struggle.

I usually close this lecture with the phrase: 'It's all good work'. I do that because I believe it, but also because I want to forestall arguments about which approach is best. I have seen social reformers spend too much of their precious time and energy fighting each other over the merits of revolution vs. reform. To me, the appropriate choice is a matter of personality rather than strategy.

It's all good work. It all needs to be done. And it cannot wait.

Changing Directions in Business Education

Knowledge Sharing for Sustainability

Suzanne Benn, Tamsin Angus-Leppan, Melissa Edwards,
Paul Brown and Stuart White
University of Technology, Sydney

Business schools are lagging other sectors in recognising the growing importance of sustainability concerns in business decision making. Many educators blame the ambiguity of sustainability-related
concepts, lack of interdisciplinary knowledge on sustainability issues
and their little training in the teaching methods needed to support
knowledge development in business sustainability. This paper
presents findings from an exploratory study of educators at one
university where sustainability is incorporated in business and other
areas of the teaching curriculum and where a community of practice
has been developed to share sustainability-related material across
the disciplinary areas. Through the lens of the boundary objects that
facilitate knowledge sharing around environmental and social
aspects of corporate sustainability, the paper discusses the barriers
and opportunities to engaging students with the new business
models of corporate sustainability.

- Business schools
- Embedding sustainability
- Interdisciplinary curriculum
- Sustainable business
- Boundary objects

Professor **Suzanne Benn**'s work spans the sciences and social sciences. She
works with colleagues at UTS Business School and across UTS to promote
sustainability. She is a specialist in education for sustainability, sustainable
business and corporate responsibility.

✉ UTS Business School, Box 123, Broadway, Sydney, NSW, 2007, Australia

🖥 Suzanne.benn@uts.edu.au

Dr **Angus-Leppan** is a qualitative researcher specializing in organizational
sustainability at UTS Business School. Her research focuses on sensemaking
and corporate sustainability.

✉ UTS Business School, Box 123, Broadway, Sydney, NSW, 2007, Australia

🖥 Tamsin.angus-leppan@uts.edu.au

Melissa Edwards is a senior lecturer at the UTS Business School since 2005,
where she specialises in sustainability management and organisation theory.
Her research focuses on sustainability, social impact, complexity and
stakeholder theories.

✉ UTS Business School, Box 123, Broadway, Sydney, NSW, 2007, Australia

🖥 Melissa.Edwards@uts.edu.au

Paul Brown is a lecturer in Accounting at UTS Business School since 2005, specializing in governance, production economics and sustainability. His research focus is how organisations can be structured and managed to be sustainable.

✉ UTS Business School, Box 123, Broadway, Sydney, NSW, 2007, Australia

🖥 Paul.j.brown@uts.edu.au

With over thirty years' experience in sustainability research, Professor **Stuart White**'s work focuses on achieving sustainability outcomes for a range of government, industry and community clients across Australia and internationally.

✉ Institute for Sustainable Futures, UTS, Box 123, Broadway, Sydney, NSW, 2007, Australia

🖥 Stuart.white@uts.edu.au

Business is being pushed to change. Issues such as income inequities, food security, ecosystem decline and climate change are confronting the current economic system and associated business models. Many businesses are responding. For example, in Australia institutional investors—especially superannuation funds—continue to lead the way, increasingly concerned with these emerging sustainability risks and the potential impact on profitability and investment returns. Recent changes include those to the ASX Corporate Governance Principles and Recommendations, affecting all listed companies with a new requirement to disclose material exposure to sustainability risks, and to report on the management of these risks. The principles of the circular economy are receiving global interest and being embraced by leading business organisations such as Unilever, Kingfisher and Cisco that represent different business sectors. Other notable examples include the increased engagement with external reporting regimes such as the Global Reporting Initiative and the Carbon Disclosure Project.

But it appears that a substantial number of business schools are lagging other sectors in this change. For example, Sundin and Wainwright (2010) found evidence for a low level of integration of sustainability into the accounting majors offered for 17 of 22 of the highest ranked universities in Australia, and with only four offering standalone subjects assessable as part of an Accounting major. Recognising the importance of business schools in shaping the future of business, this paper identifies the barriers and opportunities to business schools in embedding sustainability in their mainstream curricula. Even as corporations increasingly acknowledge notions of corporate accountability for environmental and social sustainability, business schools remain focused on teaching according to traditional business models based on concepts of competition. As a result, emergent themes such as cooperative capitalism or new business models such as those underpinning the BCorps movement are neglected in business school curricula. MBA programmes have been accused of typically including token electives on corporate social responsibility or sustainability, with little evidence that such concepts are integrated across the curriculum (Mohamed, 2014). One recent survey of business school academics found that the related topics of CSR, sustainability and sustainable development were not embedded in any coherent way in business curricula, that while most business school faculty members feel these subjects are common themes throughout departmental curricula, few feel that they are important themes and that overall, CSR, sustainability and sustainable development were not well institutionalised, with best practice still to be defined (Doh and Tashman, 2014). Recommendations were for champions such as AACSB (Association to Advance Collegiate Schools of Business) and for the use of an integrated framework in teaching these concepts (Doh and Tashman, 2014).

While other studies have taken a more positive view (e.g. Steketee, 2009), the picture remains patchy. This point is well demonstrated in another study which analysed MBA programmes according to the Sustainability Phase Model (Benn *et al.*, 2014). This model classifies approaches to sustainability in terms of Rejection; Non-Responsiveness; Compliance; Efficiency; Strategic Proactivity; and the Sustaining or Ideal Organisation phases. The study found that MBA programmes ranged from a business as usual approach (Compliance Phase), to a calculative introduction of sustainability according to market demand (Efficiency Phase), to a more systematic approach focused on incorporating sustainability into core aspects of the MBA programme (Strategic Proactivity Phase), to an MBA designed purposely around sustainability, which can be classified as at the Ideal or Sustaining Phase (Edwards and Benn, 2014).

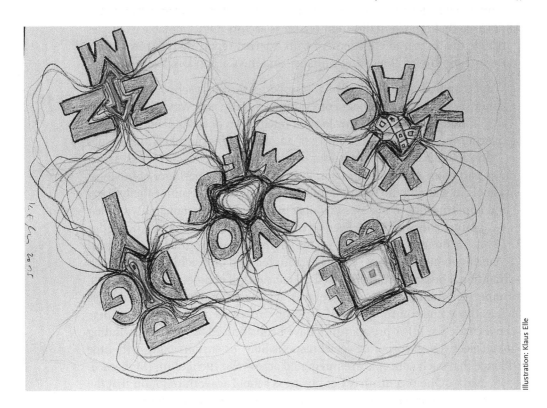

Illustration: Klaus Elle

Barriers identified to date point to a more systematic approach to integrating sustainability and to foregrounding more progressive approaches to the role of business include the ambiguity of sustainability-related concepts, lack of interdisciplinary knowledge on sustainability issues and lack of training in the teaching methods needed to support contemporary practice in business sustainability (e.g. Benn and Dunphy, 2009; Doh and Tashman, 2014; Kawaga, 2007). Organisational factors such as the lack of interest among members of the university, conflicting goals within the university, time constraints, and 'the profit orientation of the university' also contribute

(Wang *et al.*, 2010). A key problem appears to be lack of understanding in business schools of the wide range of disciplinary principles and their associated impacts that underpin sustainability and the dynamic nature of these interconnections. This leads us to suggest that providing the means for both educators and their business school students to cross disciplinary boundaries and engage with knowledge from different disciplinary areas would facilitate a systematic and integrated approach to sustainability as it is translated into the curricula and that such an approach would enable students to go beyond business as usual.

This paper presents findings from an exploratory study of educators at one university where sustainability is incorporated in business and other areas of the teaching curriculum and where a community of practice has been developed to share sustainability-related material across the disciplinary areas. Through the lens of the boundary objects in the form of concepts, models, tools and activities that facilitate knowledge sharing around environmental and social aspects of corporate sustainability, the paper discusses the barriers and opportunities to engaging students with the new business models of corporate sustainability.

Theoretical lens: boundary objects

In our research context of multiple boundaries across intersecting knowledge communities, identifying appropriate boundary objects would seem to be a way of integrating the dimensions of sustainability in a way that is coherent and meaningful to diverse participants. Boundary objects are 'artifacts, documents, terms, concepts and other forms of reification around which communities of practice can organize their interconnections' (Wenger, 1998: 105). They can be artefacts in the form of made things such as tools or visual representations or discourses, terms, concepts, processes or technologies (Star and Griesemer 1989; Wenger 2000). Basically, they have one objective manifestation, either physical or conceptual, but this manifestation is interpreted differently by different actors (Gal *et al.*, 2004).

Boundary objects allow different actors or groups or stakeholders to work together across disciplinary boundaries. They exist in different forms: the repository, such as a website or a library or a collection or a database where heterogeneity is modularised; the ideal type or general model and standardised methods, protocols and forms, including training materials which facilitate communication and the grouping of diverse content (Star & Griesemer, 1989). They can be conceptual or material.

Boundary objects are claimed as a means of changing practice through transforming knowledge across diverse or specialised knowledge or role base domains (Benn & Martin, 2010; Briers & Chua, 2004; Oswick & Robertson, 2009). As texts, boundary objects facilitate interaction across different work-related worlds. Formalisation processes create boundary objects as texts, such as minutes, diagrams, models, or charts. As texts, boundary objects also play a role in recontextualisation or the transferring and translating of knowledge (Oswick & Robertson, 2009). We argue boundary objects are particularly appropriate to consider in relation to the networks of practice that might form around sustainability education, as they allow for the tension between coordination across heterogeneous groups of actors (discipline groups) and the need for more depth and understanding in specific knowledge bases

In this paper we explore the boundary objects that might facilitate knowledge sharing around environmental and social aspects of corporate sustainability, across different tertiary education disciplines. The case is described next.

Research method and case description

The case described in this study is UTS Business School, a large business school within the University of Technology (UTS), Sydney. A number of different disciplinary areas feature sustainability teaching and research programmes across UTS, including in the business school. The business school is Association to Advance Collegiate Schools of Business (AACSB) accredited therefore needs to comply with AACSB Standard 9, requiring that teaching programmes at all levels should address 'Social responsibility, including sustainability, and ethical behaviour and approaches to management'. AACSB accreditation, according to Standard 9, involves regular self-evaluation reports, complemented by a peer review process which checks the means by which student attributes such as ability to apply sustainability-related values in their workplace, are developed through the programme. Considerable effort has gone into ensuring the prominence of sustainability within the curricula. The business school has employed senior academic staff specifically charged with the responsibility of engaging with business school faculty as well as other areas across the university to promote sustainability. A Working Party has been formed within the business school to facilitate such an outcome. A number of specific subjects have been developed that focus on managing for sustainability and corporate social responsibility, that highlight new measures for assessing social value and that highlight some core principles of ecological economics. Many educators across UTS participate in a web-based community of practice (www.sustainability.edu.au) specifically formed to share curriculum around sustainability. Hence the UTS Business School teaching programme acts as a paradigmatic case that can inform on strategies and barriers to integrating sustainability more effectively in business school programmes (See Flyvbjerg, 2006).

Data for the case was obtained from two sources. The first was a focus group conducted with educators from environmental science, management and accounting disciplines. The participating educators, a convenience sample, were chosen because they are involved with the community of practice formed around the sustainability website. As such, they are among the most dedicated to teaching sustainability at the university, and therefore best able to provide rich descriptions of their experience with teaching sustainability. The focus group questions were selected to explore the boundary objects that provide opportunity for teaching sustainability across teaching disciplines, as well as to add to the literature on barriers to the introduction of emergent sustainability themes. The website itself uses boundary objects to classify teaching materials and sustainability issues that translate across teaching disciplines, such as energy efficiency, climate and business sustainability. The focus group was transcribed verbatim and an initial thematic analysis undertaken.

The second source of data related to specific subjects taught within the business school. We reviewed online data describing the various subject objectives, content and teaching approaches and interviewed coordinators of representative subjects core to teaching programmes from the different disciplinary areas. Each subject area was written up as a specific 'case' in terms of approaches to sustainability.

Findings

Focus group findings

The focus group revealed a number of opportunities and barriers to teaching sustainable business. Key themes emerging from the focus group are set out below:

Tensions between empowerment and confrontation

Focus group participants discussed how it is difficult to teach sustainability without sounding negative, as one participant suggested, 'if you're not careful the message is constantly negative … here's all these environmental issues … doom and gloom'. Another participant suggested it is also difficult not to appear to be preaching to students and 'most people don't like what they see as being preached at. I think we could easily slide into that in any of our areas actually … the thing of being seen as a doo-gooder'.

Another participant, a management lecturer, noted the problem that students feel confronted and deflated when faced with sustainability issues at a time when they want to feel empowered about their futures:

> The reality is really confronting and really big and they want to feel empowered by their education because they are paying for it and they want to go out and get a good job and establish their careers and they are at the beginning of their lives.

A general finding from the focus group was that the educators dealt with these tensions by appealing to student self-interest as a means of adding relevance. As the environmental science educator described it:

> I try to get them see things in that very broad spectrum to say that 'a bunch of you, you're not going to end up being research scientists'. Even though we focus a lot on research where there's not many jobs. So I try to get them to think across the whole technical right through to the managerial. A lot of them are interested in management, cause they can see that is where they will really make a difference in the environment.

Another management educator argued that the tendency for business schools to focus on traditional models of organisational purpose and leadership meant that to then talk about ...

> ... things like virtues and authentic leadership, it's really confronting for them and for me and it puts me in a whole different place with them for the whole subject and that's 12 weeks with a group of students that could go completely pear-shaped.

Worldviews on business

The educators shared the view that there is little in the education system to contextualise sustainable business or to enable students to engage with wider public interest or with public policy-making, so students are not prepared for the big picture view of business that sustainability thinking requires. As one management educator said: 'Me, me, me, me as most important, me as a leader and all this stuff about what's a good leader ...? There's not enough public policy ... in any of our education in my view'.

Another participant, an environmental science educator, also commented that students do not appear to recognise that business and government each have responsibilities for sustaining the natural environment, that public policy-making needs to recognise that mix and that both science and business students will face that reality in their working lives. He talked about the perception from students that government, not business, is responsible for the environment:

> People traditionally think of environmental management being government responsibility. But when I point out the limits to the powers of the government, the amount of land on private ownership, for example, that has high conservation

value, for example, the fact that you've got to change people's behaviours to lead people to the point 'well there's got to be more than just a government responsibility there's also individuals and corporations'. That's the way I introduce it and build the idea that there is a need for it.

One management educator said 'the biggest barriers for colleagues are these fixed mental models of not just what business but what the whole capitalist system is all about' and another added 'they're very much focused on greed is good still and that is what motivates students', suggesting that educators' attitudes are reinforced by students' limited worldviews. Another participant suggested that some colleagues hold outdated views of business and sustainability and that they lack understanding of the science of specific areas such as climate change and this is the major barrier to teaching.

Cases, models, websites and activities as boundary objects for sharing knowledge

The environmental science educator used case studies from the sustainability website to demonstrate how environmental science students can support transformation in business. Talking about a particular case of a bank, which performs highly in sustainability rankings, he said:

> The data about financial savings, the reduction in waste, it's the stuff that I know as science students they can relate to much more clearly to the quantitative, when I can demonstrate the quantitative outcomes. I like the fact that it also demonstrates the power of particular individuals in an organisation to make change, as initiators of change.

This is an example where a carefully designed boundary object in the form of an archetypal sustainable business can bridge disciplinary boundaries, enabling both science and business students to share some core understandings yet use their specific knowledge bases to drill down into the case.

Several of the participants referred to their use of boundary objects such as sustainable business phase models as a means of showing students from different disciplinary areas the range of sustainability approaches and what that might mean for the HR managers, engineers and accountants who in one way or another might be involved in implementing sustainability. The circular economy was also mentioned as a model for business, which enabled students and educators from different educational backgrounds to share knowledge around some core principles but then to develop those principles further within their specialist discipline. The Sustainability Phase Model shown at Figure 1, for example, was used by educators from across the business school and from environmental science as a means of highlighting how business can be reimagined in line with sustainability.

Figure 1 Sustainability Phase Model

Source: Benn *et al.*, 2014, p. 22

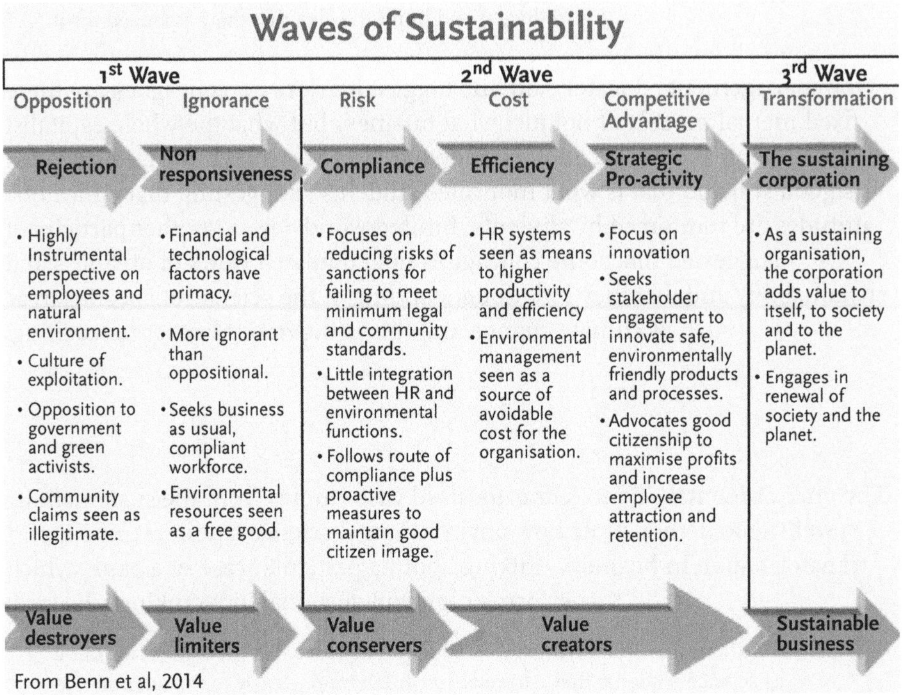

Waves of Sustainability

1st Wave		2nd Wave			3rd Wave
Opposition	Ignorance	Risk	Cost	Competitive Advantage	Transformation
Rejection	Non responsiveness	Compliance	Efficiency	Strategic Pro-activity	The sustaining corporation
• Highly Instrumental perspective on employees and natural environment. • Culture of exploitation. • Opposition to government and green activists. • Community claims seen as illegitimate.	• Financial and technological factors have primacy. • More ignorant than oppositional. • Seeks business as usual, compliant workforce. • Environmental resources seen as a free good.	• Focuses on reducing risks of sanctions for failing to meet minimum legal and community standards. • Little integration between HR and environmental functions. • Follows route of compliance plus proactive measures to maintain good citizen image.	• HR systems seen as means to higher productivity and efficiency • Environmental management seen as a source of avoidable cost for the organisation.	• Focus on innovation • Seeks stakeholder engagement to innovate safe, environmentally friendly products and processes. • Advocates good citizenship to maximise profits and increase employee attraction and retention.	• As a sustaining organisation, the corporation adds value to itself, to society and to the planet. • Engages in renewal of society and the planet.
Value destroyers	Value limiters	Value conservers	Value creators		Sustainable business

From Benn et al, 2014

A participant from the accounting discipline talked about the importance of showing students the effect of 'business as usual' to justify a need for transformation of business. He noted the importance of identifying specific boundary objects that would enable students to bridge worlds.

> Nothing quite like showing people. Like when I showed the students this thing with the workers, cause I actually set students up for this, cause you know everyone took outsourcing as this great wonderful thing, especially accountants like 'yeah! outsourcing is great yeah!' Then I say to them what does that mean? What does cost reduction mean in this context? Let's have a look and I show them the video so they are on this semi-euphoric kind of greedy state of mind and then like, you show them this absolute degradation of humanity just right in front of them as a consequence of what they said and … sometimes the students are quite shocked.

Another participant from management identified boundary objects in the form of experiential activities, 'getting students to have an emotional response to something through working through a simulated experience', as an important teaching tool for sustainability. However a participant from environmental science noted they would need support to run experiential activities related to business, highlighting the need for these objects to be co-developed across disciplinary boundaries:

I've done it in other contexts, doing experiential activities, but areas I've been very familiar with. I would need a lot of support to do one in this area. I think it's a great idea but I'd need a lot of support to be able to do it properly. To make sure I designed it properly so that they got the experience that I was aiming for.

Subject case study findings

Wicked problems as boundary objects

The available online material and the interviews with subject coordinators demonstrate a wide variability in terms of how sustainability is incorporated across the teaching programme in the business school. The leading example of a holistic approach to integration is provided by an undergraduate subject specifically designed around the purpose of bringing to bear highly coordinated trans-disciplinary understandings on a wicked problem, such as food security or climate change. In this sense, the wicked problem acts as a boundary object. Wicked problems by definition (Rittel and Webber, 1973) are problems that are difficult to solve because of the underpinning multiple, interconnected issues. Those addressed in this subject, which is a core or compulsory subject within the large undergraduate teaching programme, are specifically selected so that they highlight the interconnectedness between the different sustainability elements, then becoming the focus of the student assessments, guest lectures as well as tutorials and the more formal lectures. From a curriculum design perspective, this subject aims to make the student aware of the various theoretical frameworks for critiquing the role of business in society, while also taking a holistic approach which brings in perspectives and thinking styles from other disciplines, such as design. An important aspect of the integration is the drawing together of legal, accounting and ethical concerns into the wicked problem, with input from experts in these fields. The expectation is that students will gain the basis to develop the critical capacity to examine traditional business practices and the innovative potential to realise other business approaches and ways of looking at the world.

Energy efficiency concepts as boundary objects

Another core subject in the programme in the Accounting discipline and the stringent accreditation requirements placed by the Accounting professional associations around professional ethics mean that there is a long-term high level of compliance on ethics and ethical issues that pertain to sustainability. The subject goes beyond compliance in the extent to which it introduces concepts of energy efficiency in order to highlight reduction in resource use. Energy efficiency concepts are introduced via an emphasis on capital budgeting and student teams work on campus energy projects, thus introducing students to the interdisciplinary aspects of energy and resource use. In this subject it is the concept of energy efficiency which acts as a boundary object, enabling the bringing together of different sub-disciplinary areas to a focus on an aspect of sustainability. The coordinator for the subject is very active in sharing knowledge on the sustainability website, particularly around linking marginal abatement cost curves to sustainability models.

Discussion

Our findings confirm the importance of identifying suitable boundary objects to enable recognition of sustainability as a broad-based problem with social, environmental, economic and governance implications. This can be done through educators and students being able to access interdisciplinary materials through such boundary objects as the sustainability website, various business models or by using concepts such as the wicked problems that different lecturers can access and contribute to from their particular knowledge base. Boundary objects such as energy efficiency also link the university curricula to professional practice and provide a real world context for students who otherwise do not see the relevance of sustainability to business.

Our findings also highlight the importance of teaching so that students recognise the context of business as existing in an institutional field in which different types of organisations, such as business, government and NGOs, all play a part. Indeed, an important aspect of teaching sustainability is that it does provide students with an understanding of the complexity of current business thinking which cannot be limited to or contained within specific disciplinary boundaries.

Table 1 Summary of boundary objects used by educators to enable boundary-spanning meaning making for students

Selected boundary objects	Learning objective	Disciplinary and other boundaries traversed in the meaning making process
Case study of an archetypal sustainable business	To teach science students how they can support the transformation of businesses toward sustainability	Bridging of science and business perspectives
Sustainability phase models	To expose students to multiple perspectives on sustainable business so they are able to locate their own worldview and that of other actors, on a sustainability continuum	Human Resources, Accounting and Finance, Economics, Engineering among others

Selected boundary objects	Learning objective	Disciplinary and other boundaries traversed in the meaning making process
News report by an investigative journalist into the conditions of workers in factories supplying multinational enterprises, accessible via YouTube	To expose management accounting students to the complexity of decision-making around tradeoffs between economic, social and environmental impacts	Functional economic with humanistic/ethical perspectives
Wicked problems	To afford students the opportunity to actively engage with sustainability issues in a structured way to encourage trans-disciplinary understating and thinking	Legal, accounting, and ethical concerns in the context of complex systems and ecological concerns
The concept of 'energy efficiency'	The concept allows accounting students, who are skilled in tackling economic efficiency, to see that accountants have a role in promoting sustainable business	Engineering and management accounting perspectives

While perhaps not branded as such, we also found that boundary objects were used quite instrumentally by educators to enable boundary-spanning meaning making for students. Table 1 provides a summary of the boundary objects highlighted as useful through the study. Notably, the repertoire of boundary objects ranges from concepts such as energy efficiency or wicked problems, artefacts such as models, digital media such as videos, to activities such as role-play. Each of the boundary objects identified were used as provocations, to provide an occasion for students to see the need or possibility for boundary-spanning perspectives.

Our case study also confirms that students will not be motivated in areas that lie outside business as usual teaching programmes unless educators are given the means to address barriers to teaching sustainability such as lack of understanding of complex and interdisciplinary issues. For some educators this may stem from inexperience with contemporary business practice and certainly, as highlighted here, teachers need support to design experiential activities that demonstrate to students the thinking and concepts behind emergent models of business sustainability.

Nor do students from other disciplinary areas such as the environmental sciences appear to understand that business has the power to bring about change or how their specialised training can support such a transformation. As suggested here, sustainability problems can appear intractable and outside the responsibilities of young students focused on starting careers. However, an empowering education will provide students with the means to engage critically with the profound challenges that lie beyond traditional ideas on the role of business.

Conclusion

The aim of this study was to explore barriers and opportunities to engage students with the new business models of corporate sustainability. We found our educators faced a range of challenges, most evident in the limited world-views held by many students. Encouraging students to think about sustainability in an interdisciplinary way can itself provide a transformative learning experience whereby their world-views, values and assumptions may be challenged. When sustainability is introduced in a way that signifies how it relates to business by drawing on other disciplines it inspires students to learn and think outside of the box. Students engage positively with models that incorporate interdisciplinary knowledge, such as the circular economy and the sustainability phase model because they situate business thinking in the context of the impacts and consequences of decision-making. Through this learning process their conceptual framing of the role and purpose of business is enriched and they are more likely to start working and living more sustainably.

The findings suggest that carefully constructed and presented boundary objects can be used instrumentally to facilitate boundary-spanning knowledge sharing and creation. Given the perceived value of the identified boundary objects, the study highlights the value of communities of practice and mechanisms such as knowledge sharing websites in disseminating 'field tested' boundary objects to wider education communities. The findings also suggest that further curriculum development needs to be done to introduce business students to the science of sustainability and to systems thinking, while for science students the need is for a better understanding of the capacity of business as a driver for positive change. In short, the research highlights the need for the complementarity of different disciplinary areas across the university to be better recognised and deployed in the name of sustainable futures.

References

Benn S, and Dunphy D. (2008). 'Action research as an approach to integrating sustainability into MBA programs: An exploratory study'. *Journal of Management Education* 33(3): 276–295.

Benn, S., Dunphy, D and Griffiths, G. (2014) *Organisational Change for Corporate Sustainability*, 3rd edition, London: Routledge.

Benn, S. & Martin, A. (2010) 'Learning and Change for Sustainability Reconsidered: A Role for Boundary Objects', *Academy of Management Learning and Education*, 9, (3), 397-412.

Briers, M. & Chua, W. F. (2001). 'The role of actor-networks and boundary objects in management accounting change: a field study of an implementation of activity-based costing'. *Accounting Organizations and Society*, 26(3): 237-269.

Doh, J. P. and P. Tashman (2014). 'Half a World Away: The Integration and Assimilation of Corporate Social Responsibility, Sustainability, and Sustainable Development in Business School Curricula'. *Corporate Social Responsibility and Environmental Management* 21(3): 131-142.

Edwards, M. and Benn, S. (2014) 'The Business Case(s) for Holistic Sustainability Management Education: A Framework and Phase Model'. Professional Development Workshop, Sustainability in Management Education – Part 2: In Search of a Multidisciplinary, Innovative and Integrated Approach through University Leadership, Scholarship and Partnerships. Academy of Management Conference, Philadelphia, 2-8 August 2014.

Flyvbjerg, B. (2006) 'Five Misunderstandings about Case Study Research', *Qualitative Inquiry* 12 (2): 219- 245.

Gal, U., Yoo, Y., Boland, R.J. 2004. The Dynamics of Boundary Objects, Social Infrastructures and Social Identities. Case Western Reserve University, USA. *Sprouts: Working Papers on Information Systems*, 4(11). http://sprouts.aisnet.org/4-11

Kawaga F. (2007). 'Dissonance in students' perceptions of sustainable development and sustainability. Implications for curriculum change'. *International Journal of Sustainability in Higher Education* 8(3): 317–338.

Mohamed, E. (2014), 'The future is green for business schools', *Financial Times*, October 5 http://www.ft.com/intl/cms/s/2/c01a951c-166d-11e4-8210-00144feabdco. html#axzz3FFZFngJH accessed 23 October, 2014

Rittel, Horst W. J. and Webber, M. (1973). 'Dilemmas in a General theory of Planning. *Policy Sciences* 4: 155–169.

Star, S.L. and Griesemer, JR (1989). 'Institutional ecology, "translations" and boundary objects: amateurs and professionals in Berkeley's Museum of Vertebrate Zoology, 1907-39'. *Social Studies of Science*, 19: 387-420.

Steketee, D. (2009) 'A Million Decisions: Life on the (Sustainable Business) Frontier', *Journal of Management Education*, 33 (3): 391-401

Sundin, H. & Wainwright, L. (2010) 'Approaches to integrating social and environmental accounting (SEA) into accounting majors in Australian universities'. *Social and Environmental Accountability Journal*, 30(2): 80-95

Oswick, C. & Robertson, M. (2009) 'Boundary objects reconsidered: From bridges and anchors to barricades and mazes'. *Journal of Change Management*, 9(2): 179-194

Wang, F., Dyball, M. C. & Wright, S. (2010) 'Sustainability in an Australian University: Staff Perceptions', Sixth APIRA Conference, Sydney, Australia, July 12-13.

Wenger, E. 2000. 'Communities of Practice and Social Learning Systems' *Organization*. 7: 225-246.

Action Research as a Transformative Force in Management Education

Introducing the Collaboratory

Katrin Muff*

Business School Lausanne, Switzerland

- Action research
- Management education
- Business schools
- Vision 50+20
- Business sustainability
- Doctorate in business administration (DBA)
- Business education
- The Collaboratory

This article examines the potential for scalability of action research in the domain of management education. It considers the individual, the institutional as well as the systemic perspective of embracing action research and provides telling examples in all three domains. Using the guiding framework of the seven choice points of quality action research (from clarifying objectives, working in partnership with stakeholders, through to cultivating stakeholder reflexivity), the article seeks to establish a link between existing best practices in action research with applied transformational processes in management education. The widely recognised 'Vision 50+20' (www.50plus20. org) sets the stage for the challenge at hand and is used as a framework to define the scope. The three roles defined in the Vision 50+20 call for compelling examples of action research. These roles cover two existing responsibilities of business schools, educating globally responsible leaders and research that enables business to serve the common good; as well as an additionally defined role concerning the transformation of economy and society. Last but not least, the author seeks to inspire further research and discussion in this domain.

Katrin Muff serves as Dean of Business School Lausanne since 2008. Under her leadership, the school embraced sustainability, responsibility and entrepreneurship in a three pillar vision. Her international business experience includes nearly a decade with Alcoa in Europe, the US and in Russia. She worked for Iams Pet Food as Strategic Planning Director and has co-founded a European incubator for early-seed start-ups. Muff researches in the interdisciplinary domains of education, business sustainability and leadership. She has co-founded the World Business School Council for Sustainable Business and is actively engaged in GRLI's project 50+20, a vision of management education for the world.

✉ Rte de la Maladière 21, PO Box 73, CH-1022, Chavannes, Switzerland

🖳 katrin.muff@bsl-lausanne.ch

---

* The final, definitive version of this paper will be first published as a chapter in the forthcoming publication *The SAGE Handbook of Action Research* (3rd edition), SAGE Publications Ltd, and is reprinted in the *Building Sustainable Legacies Journal* with permission from SAGE Publications Ltd.

Broadening the use of action research in management education: clarifying objectives

Looking back at the experience of the organisational and programme transformations at Business School Lausanne (BSL), it occurs to me that action research has been, in many ways, the underlying mode of inquiry we'd been working with even before we knew it. As such, action research may be said to have revealed itself to me as a way to conceive of and further cultivate our daily work.

At BSL we have experienced so many different, at first hidden, domains of action research. In this section we will consider a number of these to demonstrate the various applications of action research. This section therefore illustrates what Bradbury-Huang (2013) refers to as the choice points of quality in action research:

▷ How we have used action research to transform the BSL organisational system as a whole

▷ How we include action research in helping companies in their transformative sustainability journey

▷ How we built on the action research philosophy to co-create a new Executive programme

▷ How to explicitly use action research as a leading future-relevant methodology in newly designed doctoral programme

▷ How to use action research to support societal change through stakeholder-engaged prototyping

Our first exposure to action research was back in my first year as Dean of BSL, when I initiated the radical re-design of our MBA programme. My coaching and consulting background had provided me with a worldview that has resulted in a preferred way to approach the creation of a new programme. It may be called a consultative collaborative approach. I called it 'stumbling forward together'. Professor Kassarjian of Babson College observed this process from the outside and wrote a three-part case study on change leadership about these initial years at BSL (Kassarjian, 2012).

When re-designing our MBA programme, our chief objective and desire was to build a programme that was in line with the expectations of the market. This meant that we needed to take a look outside to understand what the requirements were. This was contrary to the existing belief of how to construct a programme. A key element of success was the creation of an ongoing 'safe space' for exploring new ideas. We defined the needs of the market by asking how senior executives in a variety of industry define the skills, competencies and attitudes of the most valuable pearls in their organisations. Interviews with 30 CEOs and HR Directors provided us with 78 attributes and three clear priorities for the programme. The design team consisting of existing faculty, external consultants and advisers worked together to create a first prototype of the new programme which was tested by a student cohort and further improved in the following two years. I have outlined this process in detail (Muff, 2012).

After a further two years, we gathered again and considered the extensive feedback of students and embraced new important design changes in the programme. We are currently in the third ongoing re-design phase and both students and professors have come to appreciate the ongoing dialogue around how we can further improve the programme to reach our objective.

An important thing we learned when *articulating these objectives* is that the quality in what we did, and in action research in general, is reflected 'in the extent to which the action research explicitly addresses the objectives relevant to the work and the choices made in meeting those' (Bradbury-Huang, 2013). We learned that again and again, we needed to clarify our underlying worldviews and perspectives to unveil subconscious intentions.

Partnership & participation: turning BSL into a co-creative platform

As a privately owned, relatively small business school, BSL represents a unique opportunity to advance the agenda of providing responsible and sustainable education to future leaders in business and beyond. In the past two years, we have used the evaluation and auditing process of the Economy of the Common Good movement (ECG) to re-energise our transformational process. The ECG originated in Austria (www.gemeinwohl-oekonomie. org) and builds on the key constitutional values of dignity, solidarity, ecological sustainability, social justice, and democracy, to create a matrix for organisations to evaluate their contribution to society based on how these values are translated for all relevant stakeholders.

To re-vitalise the transformative spirit, we chose to have students drive the project and applied for a paid consulting project in the Executive Diploma in Sustainable Business that we jointly operate with the University of St Gallen. For 10 months, a team of four students led the process of evaluating BSL's societal contribution through extensive engagement with all stakeholder groups (students, parents, alumni, companies, the board, the administration and the faculty). Once they had identified the blind spots, the students invited representatives of all stakeholders to brainstorm how we could overcome these blind spots. Nine so-called 'green-teams' formed, consisting of always a mix of stakeholders, often students, professors and administrative staff. Over a period of 6 to 12 months, these teams worked to implement important changes at BSL, creating a dynamic and a spirit of change unlike anything the organisation had ever experienced. The entry-hall was redone, plastic cups eliminated, awareness videos shot and most importantly, a new mission was developed and born that has since propelled BSL to fully embrace the three-pillared vision simultaneously: sustainability–responsibility–entrepreneurship.

In this stakeholder-driven process to define our mission, my fear was that the end result would be a consensus-driven, watered-down, weak, pleasing statement that wouldn't contain the seeds of provocation and rebellion that we were starting to dare to express more fully. Interestingly, the opposite happened. Once first drafts started to circulate and the debate about the message was launched, some of the more conservative stakeholders—our faculty—surprised us all by fully embracing what we had in mind. I remember very keenly a moment when a professor of marketing said in a large circular discussion:

> If you really want to be that radical and if you are not afraid of what this means to your customers and market, then you need to be a lot more explicit and clear about it. Express it loud and clear; at least this will enable those that get it to be attracted to the school.

I am very proud of our mission which now reads: 'We provide a learning platform for individuals and organizations to thrive by co-creating viable business solutions for our planet and its people.' It took months to find these words. And in these months, not only friendships were built as a result of such intense *partnership and participation*, but we also experienced the broad spectrum of working with stakeholders in consultation all the way to truly engaging with them as full co-researchers in our journey.

Significance & sustainability: creating a larger vision

Ever since the financial crisis in 2008, the same year I became Dean at BSL, public voices questioning the relevance of business schools could no longer be ignored. The 50+20 movement (www.50plus20.org) emerged from a side event of the 2010 Academy of Management Annual Meeting in Montreal. The conference was attended by more than 12,000 management scholars and was held under the motto 'Daring to Care'. A handful of Deans, Directors and Professors got together to agree that it was high time that the business school community would engage in the public discussion concerning business and the economy in view of the sustainability challenges our planet and its societies were facing. And, more importantly, that it was high time that we developed a radical new vision for business schools and management education as a whole. The story of what followed is well documented, covering the collaborative visioning process and the launch activities at the

Illustration: Klaus Elle

RIO+20 Conference in June 2012 (e.g. Muff, 2013). The 50+20 vision, which can be summarised as follows, became the guiding star for BSL:

Rather than train managers for organisations that operate within 20th century logic, management educators need to answer the call of service to become custodians which provide a service to society. The management school of the future understands that transforming business, the economy and society begins with its own internal transformation. Thus becoming an example by *being the change* such an institution wishes to progress, Vision 50+20 envisions three fundamental roles in management education:

1. **Educating** and developing globally responsible leaders

2. **Enabling** business organisations to serve the common good

3. **Engaging** in the transformation of business and the economy

As a primary educational institution, our prime focus was to improve and transform our educational programmes. In addition, however, the 50+20 vision made us realise that we could and should embrace our responsibility in helping the transformation of organisations both in business and beyond to embrace sustainability, thus serving society and the planet. Our greatest challenge was to embrace the newly defined role of becoming a meeting place for citizens and concerned stakeholders to resolve burning societal issues. Having been instrumental in developing the 'Collaboratory' methodology for 50+20 Vision, we decided to further develop and explore the range of applications of the Collaboratory.

The Collaboratory method represents an interesting way to unite all three roles defined by Vision 50+20. In the domain of education, the degree of engagement in learning can be portrayed as shown in Figure 1.

Figure 1 The evolution of teaching and learning approaches in business schools over time

Source: Muff, 2013

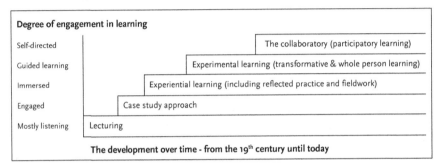

Simply put, the Collaboratory offers the highest degree of engagement of any educational tool known in business education to date. Interestingly, the Collaboratory is not only an educational tool but also a stakeholder-engagement methodology from applied research and potentially an action research practice.

A similar logic applies when considering what it might take to transform business schools. We differentiate between three orders of implementing change as illustrated in Figure 2.

Figure 2 Three orders of implementing change and learning for globally responsible leadership

Source: Muff, 2013

The three orders of implementing change in learning	Enabler 1: Transformative learning	Enabler 2: Issue-centered learning	Enabler 3: Reflective practice and fieldwork
1st order change: Bolt-on solutions	Clearly distinct isolated approaches	Clearly distinct isolated approaches	Clearly distinct isolated approaches
2nd order change: Built-in solutions	Combination of approaches		
		Combination of approaches	
3rd order change: Platform solutions	An integrated realization of the vision by using a collaboratory process		

First order change is represented by so-called 'bolt-on' solutions which can be adopted relatively easily without a deep institutional change. Second order change represents solutions which are considered 'built-in' and which demand a profound inner transformation of an institution. Third order change involves so-called 'platform' solutions which are co-created by relevant stakeholders on issues of concern. Such platform solutions exceed the existing organisational thinking and the often existing competitive spirit between institutions and aims at creating a space where collaboration can reign in service of solving an issue or concern that is of greater interest. When looking at the landscape of business schools, the biggest challenges right now are not in the area of shifting to a third order change but to recognise that a first order change has not yet really addressed the issue, no matter how challenging it was to get it accomplished.

When shifting the perspective from the institutional transformation that is required of a business school to consider what kind of support business organisations require to be able to change themselves, a similar challenge emerges. While the large majority of organisations are busy with first order change, the challenge lies not only in embedding sustainability deeply in the organisation as is defined by a second order change, but to adopt an entirely new perspective on one's purpose and become a positive contributor to solving burning societal and environmental issues in 'platform' solutions together with other relevant stakeholders (third order change). Differentiating between these three ways of thinking and operating is also a useful framework to help business organisations to understand the transformative journey to serve the common good, helping them understand what 'business sustainability' actually meant. The term sustainability had been used (and abused) increasingly in the past decade and had come to mean many things to many people. Together with Thomas Dyllick from the University of St Gallen, we developed a 'Business Sustainability Typology' defining three different types or stages for organisations to embed sustainability (Dyllick and Muff, 2013). This typology consists of three types of Business Sustainability, 1.0, 2.0 and 3.0, which can be directly connected to the three orders of change. To ensure a practical application of this conceptual idea for business, we wrote a follow-on article to facilitate the translation of the concept to the various organisational dimensions (Muff and Dyllick, 2014).

The above illustrations seek to demonstrate how an organisation of any kind can achieve *significance and sustainability* by selecting a perspective of meaning and relevance that goes beyond the immediate context of the organisation in order to support the 'flourishing of persons, communities, and the wider ecology' (Bradbury-Huang, 2013).

Actionability: co-creating future-relevant education

In the context of the 50+20 vision creation process, we felt it was important to not only propose a conceptual vision, but to also offer a concrete solution for one of the key aspects of the 50+20 vision, namely creating a sustainable business course for mid-career professionals. Given BSL's unique ability to implement new programmes swiftly, we decided to co-create such a programme in Switzerland. In the design stage, we were looking for clarity in defining the purpose and focus of the course, the learning outcomes and creative pedagogical solutions to ensure that these objectives could be achieved.

The first challenge was to identify all key stakeholders who had the relevant knowledge and experience to contribute to such a unique 'light-house' course. We invited all relevant programme directors of fellow universities, key consultants in the domain of business sustainability, coaches and facilitators experienced in developing transformative leaders to two creative brainstorming sessions which we hosted at BSL. Walls covered in paper, we facilitated a carefully designed process that helped clarify the core design principles of the programme (see Figs 3 and 4).

Figure 3 The three subject domains of the Diploma in Sustainable Business
Source: www.bsl-lausanne.ch

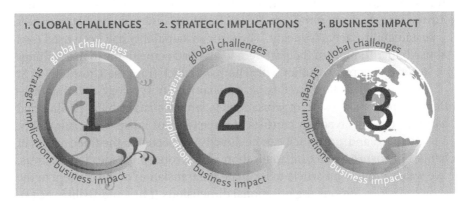

The subject competence is divided in the three aspects: starting with global challenges, from which we derive strategic implications on a societal/ industry level, to finally evaluate the business impact on an organisational level. We developed nine modules rotating through these three aspects in three consecutive rounds in order to ensure that students would end up with a fluency to shift among these different perspectives. In addition, the subject competence is complemented with leadership modules to ensure that students have the capability to implement change, and a 9-month hands-on strategic consultancy project so that graduates have applied what they have learned in a real company.

In fall 2012, we launched an innovation cohort which completed the 9-month programmes just days before we headed to the RIO+20 conference. The inclusion of the class in the programme design review and their constructive contributions to amend and improve the programme proved so valuable, that we have kept the co-creative spirit of programme design with every new class. So far, we have amended the programme three times and have always found important ways to further improve both elements and the overall structural logic. We are now in the fourth edition and have found a way to integrate the feedback of the cohorts into the ongoing design changes.

Figure 4 The three learning dimensions of the Diploma in Sustainable Business
Source: www.bsl-lausanne.ch

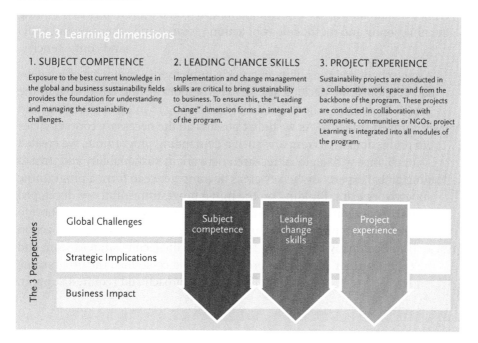

The ongoing co-creative programme design of this programme is an example of how action research can trigger and influence *actionability* as an emergent unfolding, which as Bradbury-Huang (2013) suggests highlights the ways in which: 'quality can be reflected in the extent to which the action research provides new ideas that guide action in response to need'.

Appropriate methods & process: co-creating future-relevant research

As shown, it is possible to design an educational programme in a co-creative action research manner, with stakeholders in cycles of action and reflection. Another challenge is how to reinvent the research domain in higher education. Following the launch of the 50+20 vision, the community of involved business schools challenged itself to come up with a prototype in doctoral education with the idea to develop a research faculty for the future. We started a series of meetings to discuss the objectives of an ideal doctoral training and identified the need to not only develop research skills but to also work on the person and leadership, coaching and consulting skills. After two co-creative sessions which were similar in approach to that described above, we had developed a skeleton of a programme. A key insight of these design sessions was the understanding that we needed to develop future-relevant faculty and consultants with the necessary skills to help organisations to embed sustainability. We understood that we could achieve this by adopting the philosophy and methodology of action research and other relevant skills and competencies.

As no school had the ability to quickly implement a prototype of what we had developed, we decided at BSL to revise our existing DBA programme and to launch an innovation cohort consisting of interested existing and newly enrolled students. As we didn't possess all the necessary competencies to professionally accompany such a demanding programme, we created an alliance with a global research network in sustainability and invited leading global experts in the key areas of competence to form a programme supervisory team. Building on the initial programme draft, we developed the DBA programme structure (see Fig. 5) and invited the first cohort to a one-week training session in Switzerland to provide training in action research and company consulting. In this week, the faculty support team and the cohort further refined the programme and co-defined the programme deliverables, approach and required support.

Figure 5 BSL Doctorate in Business Administration programme overview

Source: www.bsl-lausanne.ch

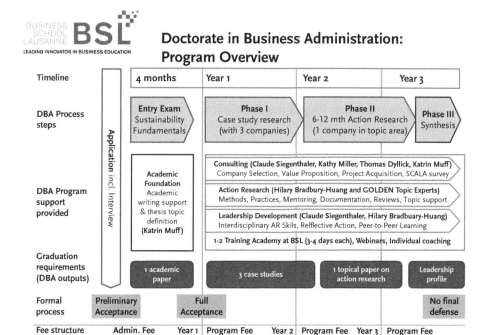

The interesting part of the journey is how the faculty and the students advance together in frequent webinars and how the support faculty co-develops the programme as we go embracing challenges such as building bridges between a more classical case-study research in phase 1 with the action research approach in phase 2. As a faculty support team, we are very conscious to what degree the continuous development and adaptation of the programme structure itself is emergent action research.

We have learned that principles of action research can be applied both in the ongoing adaptation and co-creation of a programme. Additionally they can be used as a research method and learning journey for the students in a programme. Finding the *appropriate methods and processes* in such a journey is a continuous challenge. This example seeks to serve as an illustration of how to 'articulate and illustrate the action research process and related methods, including the voices of participants in the research' (Bradbury-Huang, 2013).

Contribution to action research theory & practice: co-creating future-relevant societal engagement

When implementing the third role of the 50+20 vision, namely embracing societal engagement, we benefited from the Collaboratory philosophy and methodology that we had drafted for the RIO+20 conference and which has been very successfully used in many other applications ever since. The spontaneous spreading of the Collaboratory methodology worldwide has encouraged us to put together a practitioner handbook ('The Collaboratory'; Muff, 2014) consisting of the various underlying action research philosophies (open space, Theory U [see also Scharmer and Kaufer, in this volume], the circle work, Appreciative Inquiry [see also Graham, in this volume], etc.) and a wide variety of concrete applications in various domains (education, business, citizen movements).

A Collaboratory can be described as 'the preferred place for stakeholders to meet' (Muff, 2013). The philosophy of the Collaboratory is diametrically opposed to the thinking behind the lecture theatre and provides an open space for a broad group of stakeholders to meet on equal terms, where the teacher is replaced by a skilled facilitator. As such, the Collaboratory offers an influential alternative for public debate and problem solving, inclusive of views from business and management faculty, citizens, politicians, entrepreneurs, people from various cultures and religions, the young and the old.' It is a combination of action learning and action research as practice for large scale change endeavours.

At BSL, we use the Collaboratory as our way to engage with our local civil society. We regularly organise issue-based Collaboratory events which we hope initiate and trigger change initiatives locally. In 2012, we started with a Collaboratory on the topic of 'basic income', the idea that every citizen in need receive a basic revenue that allows her to survive. We invited all concerned stakeholders, those for and against this, those who didn't know and wanted to inform themselves, policy makers, unemployed youngsters, artists with irregular income, managers and self-employed entrepreneurs, and selected five experts among them who represented all key points of view. We measured the position of all participants at the beginning and the end of the event and were amazed to note a shift from 20% for, 80% undecided, 10% against the idea at the beginning of the session shifting to 70% for the idea, 25% undecided and 5% against the idea at the end of the session. Rarely had we seen such a powerful shift of not only awareness but revised points of view. In 2013, we held a series of Collaboratories around the idea of the 'Economy for the Common Good', an Austrian initiative that offers an alternative economic perspective and a concrete tool for organisations to measure their societal impact (Felber, 2013). The goal of this Collaboratory was to establish the Economy for the Common Goods movement locally in the Swiss French region. In 2014, we added two more Collaboratory initiatives, one on the hot issue of corruption and a student-led project on reducing consumer food waste in Switzerland by 50% in 2017. These Collaboratories have shaped our understanding of our role in the regional society and how we use the convening power of our business school to invite concerned citizens and stakeholders to meet and discuss quantum-leap solutions by back-casting from a shared vision. Participants tell us that it is impossible to explain what the experience is like unless you participate in such a facilitated process. The 'Collaboratory' book hopefully serves as a tool to grow the use of this wonderful methodology beyond its manifold applications today.

From an action research perspective, the interesting thing about the Collaboratory lies in the fact that the research topic is defined together with stakeholders and that the researcher assumes an active role in supporting prototype solutions by ensuring rigour in the implementation process of prototypes. The researcher takes an active part in the experiment and serves as both a loyal and stringent observer on how the experiment unfolds noting how assumptions, worldviews and perspectives shift in the course of the development of a prototype, as well as by providing relevant pragmatic research methodologies and tools that allow a rigorous observation of the experiment against the initially expected outcome. As such, the researcher puts himself at the service of solving a burning societal issue in real time, allowing for a very direct positive impact for society. Such a researcher operates in a very different mode than a conventional researcher who self-selects his research topic and focuses on past occurrences to understand the phenomenon he is studying. Albert Einstein once said that 'you cannot solve a problem with the same mind that created it' framing precisely the challenge and limitation of traditional research. Our interest in the Collaboratory as a tool to solve future-relevant issues with co-creative stakeholder engagement processes which as accompanied by forward-thinking action researchers is to overcome this very limitation. We consider the Collaboratory as a place where action learning meets action research. We are only starting this journey and are looking for testimonials and feedback from any action researcher with experience or an interest in furthering this field.

In summary, the Collaboratory represents not only an exciting new way to combine education and research in the relevant 'action' mode for future solutions, but it offers also an opportunity of a third-order change in business schools by advancing from 'bolt-on solutions (first-order change)' to 'built-in solutions (second-order change)' to 'platform solutions' (Muff, 2013). At such a stage, a business school or university is...

...willing to see things differently, to change its perspective and assumption and to open up to the experience of seeing its *own* worldview rather than seeing *with* its worldview. Learning processes are thus created to facilitate the fundamental recognition of a given paradigm, in order to enable paradigmatic reconstructions. These are, by definition, transformative. The challenge we see for future business schools is the transformation of the current model where a few selective owners of knowledge disseminate knowledge to the masses, to a collaborative space of shared learning. This is indeed new ground for business schools and involves innovation and creativity in its conception, design, implementation and continuous improvement (Muff, 2013).

The manifold use and application of action research as the ideal mode of research in such a collaborative space is expected to richly **contribute to the action research theory and knowledge**, hopefully enriching and expanding the vibrant community that engages with it.

Reflexivity: sharing learning among students

Bringing this home to the local student experience are Fred, Gulen and Munif, all doctoral level candidates at BSL. Across 10 time zones, they settle into their weekly Skype call updating each other on their progress with their in-company research. Fred is a master of time management and adaptability. As a busy Sales Director in charge of Europe and Asia for a US multinational, he travels 80% of his time, dialling in from the strangest places. His issue right now is to find a way to help the Head of Sustainability of a Swiss bank to convince their Head of Communications to embrace the opportunity to do a case study with him. Munif, originally from the Pacific Islands, now living in Sydney Australia, is of great support to him. He has nearly a decade of international consulting experience, building on a very successful corporate career both in Europe and Australia.

Munif:

Fred, they are afraid of potential risks involved and what might be exposed of them. It is important that the communication folks understand that nothing will be published without their prior approval. Is there a way that you can have a direct connection with these guys, even if just by phone or Skype?

Munif himself is very familiar with the challenges of long-distance consulting. All of the companies he is working with are located in Denmark—10 time zones away. He has just co-authored an important document commissioned by the Danish Government that envisions the inclusion of externalities in corporate accounting—the topic of passion for Munif. He is in a good space right now as this report not only provides him with additional exposure and credibility but also serves as an accelerator of his cause.

Fred:

That's a great idea, Munif, I'll see if I can directly talk to the communications folks and find out what their issues are. Congratulations, by the way, on your report. I am really impressed. Have you thought about how you can use it as a lever for your discussions with your companies? Have they read it yet?

Gulen, who commutes between Romania (work), Turkey (family) and the UK (research) joins in: 'Munif, great job on the report—really, hats off!' She is passionate about the well-being or social aspect of sustainability and is working with three leading hotel groups in the UK and Scandinavia to identify how to embrace well-being more fully in the hospitality industry.

> Guys, I just got the survey results from two hotels. They are really telling a great story and allow me to pin point both blind spots and areas of opportunities for the hotels. I know that the hotels are very sensitive about being compared among themselves, each fearing to look bad. I am thinking of waiting with my comparative study until later in the process and first work with each of them individually, so that we can build trust and they can get a feeling of where they stand. I am planning to finalise this approach tomorrow.

Gulen rarely asks for advice, she really knows what she is doing and is very well organised. She nonetheless enjoys being able to share her progress with her colleagues. Putting ideas into words and speaking them out loud has helped her tremendously to gain clarity.

Reflexivity is a key and *choice point* in doing good action research. Not only Gulen, but also Fred and Munif are learning to appreciate the friendship that has developed between them, but also that their peer learning is an opportunity to continuously re-clarify their own roles, the context and the underlying reason for their involvement with the companies that have engaged in action research with them. Their weekly call is one example of what allows them to take a self–critical stance and to see how their perspective limits or contributes to the creation of knowledge. It is also augmented by coaching from their faculty team as well as the use of the Global Leadership Profile to develop self-insight and aspirations with regard to first person action research.

The seven choice points of action research quality

Using the structure of the seven quality choice points of action research (Bradbury, 2013), we highlighted a wide range of applications for action research. At BSL, we have used the action research methodology as a philosophy of co-creation at all levels: at the strategic level of BSL (section 3), as an organisational tool for transformation (section 4), as a means to co-create new forms of education (section 5) as well as new forms of research (section 6), to ultimately support the Collaboratory idea which serves as a means to engage in resolving societal issues by combining a stakeholder engagement process with action learning and action research (section 7).

Figure 6 Connecting article sections with action research quality points

#	Sub-section	AR choice point
1	Broadening the use of action research	Articulation of objectives
2	Turning BSL into a platform of co-creation	Partnership & participation
3	Creating a larger vision	Significance & sustainability
4	Co-creating future-relevant education	Actionability
5	Co-creating future-relevant research	Appropriate methods & process
6	Co-creating future-relevant societal engagement	Contribution to AR theory-practice
7	Sharing learning among students	Reflexivity

We may well only have seen the tip of the iceberg in the endless opportunities of applying action research as a driver for future-relevant transformation at all levels of change: the individual, the organisational and the societal level. Further research is required to explore this emerging field of broad application of action research and we welcome contributions, testimonials and ideas of how to advance further.

Bibliography

Bradbury-Huang, H. (2013), 'The seven choice points in action research', for the BSL DBA program, used in peer review at Action Research http://arj.sagepub.com

Dyllick, T., Muff, K. (2013), 'Clarifying the meaning of business sustainability: introducing a typology from business-as-usual to true business sustainability', in review process at the Journal for Organization & Development, SAGE Publication, a summary extract is available on SSRN http://ssrn.com/abstract=2368735

Felber, C (2012), 'Die Gemeinwohl-Ökonomie, Eine demokratische Alternative wächst', updated and extended new edition, Zsolnay

Kassarjian, J.B. (2012), 'BSL, a business school in transition', cases A, B, C, epilogue, teaching notes and teaching material, published by Babson College, available through the Case Center http://www.thecasecentre.org/educators/search/results?s=6B8477EA D2DB7F9FB69DE707B5F7A216

Muff, K. (2013). Rethinking management education for the world: A TEDx event in Lausanne, June 2013 http://youtu.be/jvipxPqS_38

Muff K., Dyllick D., Drewell M., North J., Shrivastava P. & Haertle J. (2013): *Management Education for the World: A vision for business schools serving people and planet.* Northampton: Edward Elgar.

Muff, K. (2012), 'Are business schools doing their job?', Journal of Management Development, Vol 31, Issue 7, 642-662.

Muff, K. (2013), Developing globally responsible leaders in business schools, Journal of Management Development, Vol. 32 Issue 5, pp.487-507

Muff, K. (ed.) (2014), 'The Collaboratory', Greenleaf Publishing, Sheffield, UK.

Muff, K., Dyllick T., (2014), 'An organizational roadmap towards business sustainability', available on SSRN http://ssrn.com/abstract=2442211

Purpose at the Heart of Strategy

Creating a Sustainable Business while Solving the World's Challenges

Gabi Zedlmayer

Vice President and Chief Progress Officer, HP

Companies that shift their thinking about sustainability from a sideline activity to one that's embedded in their business strategy ignite new opportunities for growth. Often companies make this shift when faced with an organisational crisis, such as risks to their supply chain or a financial crisis. Rather than wait for crisis to strike, business leaders should recognise that a purpose-driven strategy is their path to long-term sustainable growth. Integrating sustainability into the heart of a business inspires game-changing innovation, progressive problem solving, and highly engaged and motivated employees. By driving a collective shift to purpose-driven business strategy, we can accelerate the transition to a more sustainable economy as we solve society's toughest challenges.

- Sustainability
- Business strategy
- Purpose-driven strategy
- Living Progress
- Sustainable innovation
- Information technology

Gabi Zedlmayer is Vice President and Chief Progress Officer at HP. She drives HP's Living Progress initiatives, aligned with HP's business strategy, that help improve the communities we serve. She leads a global team of experts focused on solving social and environmental issues in collaboration with non-profit organisations, governments, customers, and partners. Her goal is to create solutions that improve communities and advance human, economic and environmental progress. Zedlmayer serves as a member of the board of directors of Hewlett-Packard GmbH Germany. She is also President of the Women's Council of HypoVereinsbank UNICREDIT and a member of the EU Commission e-skills leadership board.

livingprogress@hp.com

Every generation has had an industry that changed the fabric of society. Over the last 40 years, information technology (IT) has been that defining industry. It has changed not just business processes and personal productivity, but the very ways people communicate and collaborate as well.

People's increasing desire for anytime, anywhere access has been fed by the emergence of mobile devices and enabled by cloud computing. This shift to an always-connected world is creating an explosive growth in digital content—what the IT industry calls 'big data' (Fig. 1).

Figure 1 The shift to an always-connected world is creating an explosive growth in digital content

Big doesn't begin to describe the amount of data the world generates in a day. In fact, Ernst & Young (EY, 2014) reports that the world will create as much data in 10 minutes as in all of human history up until the year 2003. DOMO (James, 2014) estimates that every minute, Facebook users share nearly 2.5 million pieces of content, and Twitter users tweet 277,000 times. Those numbers are only going to multiply exponentially as new technologies, like immersive computing and wearable devices, make generating and sharing content even more pervasive.

With an increasing global population and a rising middle class in emerging economies like China, India, Indonesia, Vietnam, Thailand, and Malaysia, billions more people will be connecting in the coming decade, shifting the centres of power in the world and further accelerating the data explosion.

All that data is collected, processed, stored, and managed in large-scale data centres around the world, which collectively consume a tremendous amount of energy. Today, data centres that power the public cloud use more energy than the country of Japan (HP Labs, 2014), and may soon require more energy than we can even produce each year.

Illustration: Klaus Elle

As a society, we are depleting our natural resources at an alarming rate. According to the Global Footprint Network, each year we already use 50% more resources than the Earth can regenerate annually; and it's projected that by 2030 we will need the equivalent of two Earths to support the planet's population if current consumption trends continue. We, of course, only have one Earth, which is why HP Chairman and CEO Meg Whitman says, 'Business as usual is not sustainable'.

> **HP Chairman and CEO Meg Whitman says, 'Business as usual is not sustainable'**

Clearly, we have to think and act differently in the way we conduct business. And the time for action is now.

Sustainable business, sustainable world

Companies like Unilever and HP have embraced this opportunity to firmly embed purpose into the heart of their business strategy. This integration is essential not only for society, but for long-term business growth, fuelling the transition to a sustainable economy.

What drives a company to adopt a purpose-driven strategy varies, but generally there are two ways companies come to adopt such strategies. For some companies, sustainability-related products or services are the reason they exist—think alternative energy companies and businesses driving the sharing economy. But other companies adopt this strategy out of urgency and necessity, perhaps resulting from risks to their supply chain or financial challenges.

Illustration: Klaus Elle

For HP, it was largely driven by our company turnaround strategy. While sustainability has been embedded in HP's DNA from the beginning, it wasn't always completely intertwined with the business strategy. That changed when we began looking at sustainability as an untapped business asset. Our leadership recognised that to optimise its value, sustainability couldn't be something we did alongside our business—it had to be core to our business strategy. In this way, HP could drive sustainable growth while solving the world's toughest challenges.

In 2013, HP launched Living Progress (Fig. 2), which is our framework for thinking about how we do business. To us it means creating a better future for everyone through our actions and innovations. We do this by working to develop the most resource-efficient IT products and services through the most responsible value chain.

Figure 2 Living Progress framework

Resource-efficient products and services

Putting purpose at the heart of strategy inspires companies to think differently about innovation; to reach beyond incremental improvements to create transformative solutions; to confront biases and constraints that obscure possibilities; and to connect customer needs with human, economic, and environmental impact. The result can be game-changing innovation that creates new market opportunities.

> **solutions must not just make incremental improvements; they must truly solve the challenges to enable sustainable growth**

While trends in mobility, social media, big data, and cloud—what we call the New Style of IT—create tremendous opportunities for technology companies like HP, our solutions must not just make incremental improvements; they must truly solve the challenges to enable sustainable growth. For example, the energy and space constraints that threaten the future of data centres is not a problem we can afford to simply slow down by making technology a little smaller or a little more efficient. We must completely rethink the way technology is delivered.

For HP, this type of innovation is imperative for the sustainability and competitiveness of our own business—and for the stability and growth of the global economy. Data fuels human and economic progress. We must find new ways of meeting the explosive demand for data using less space and energy resources to enable business to continue to function and thrive.

Figure 3 Innovations like HP Moonshot are needed to revolutionise the space and energy economics of the data centre

This is our mindset as we work to revolutionise the space and energy economics of the data centre. Today it shows up in innovations like HP Moonshot servers (Fig. 3), which delivers right-size computing for the right workloads. For example, for big data applications, the HP Moonshot solution would utilize up to 90% less power, use 97% less space, and cost 78% less than a traditional server environment.[1] And the HP Apollo 8000 System, a liquid-cooled supercomputer that can help organisations eliminate up to 3,800 tonnes of carbon dioxide waste from data centres per year.[2] Moreover, we are focused on a transformative innovation we call 'The Machine' that will redefine how we think about computing in this big data era—creating new solutions that are orders of magnitude faster, that use the optimal amount of energy for the task, and that are built at a fraction of the size.

This is the kind of creative innovation and progressive problem solving that comes from a purpose-driven strategy. For HP, we know the greatest impact we can have on driving a sustainable economy is through our product use—reducing the carbon impact of our products, replacing outdated, inefficient processes with more sustainable technology, and providing the underserved people of our world with access to resources that improve their lives and livelihoods. But we also know that just as important as what we do, is how we do it.

---

1 HP Internal testing, compared to a traditional 2U/2P rack server.
2 HP internal estimate comparing HP Apollo 8000 to an air-cooled data centre with 3 megawatts of IT. A standard sustainability formula was used to derive CO_2 savings in tonnes using the kWh savings based on real-world data centre analysis.

Most responsible value chain

> companies must take responsibility across their entire value chain and help drive human, economic and environmental progress

To make a sustainable impact and continue fuelling our world's economy, we believe companies must take responsibility across their entire value chain and help drive human, economic, and environmental progress.

With one of the most expansive supply chains in the IT industry, we work diligently to improve the resiliency and reduce the risks, while protecting the health and well-being of the workers that support that entire chain.

Since more than half of our final assembly manufacturers are located in China, this has been an area of great focus at HP. Like other global businesses operating in China, a majority of our work was focused in coastal cities, like Shanghai and Beijing. More and more workers from the countryside were forced to commute to the coast for work, and we were aware of the stress commuting was having on these workers and their families. In addition, we recognised that consolidating our manufacturing facilities in a single geographic area was exposing us to greater risk, particularly in terms of labour shortages. For these reasons, HP worked with the Chinese Government to establish a manufacturing centre in Chongqing in central China, nearer to many of the workers' homes.

This strategy, which we called Go West, can help lessen stress on workers by keeping people closer to their families, according to a *New York Times* video report. In addition, housing facilities for the workers, which resemble a typical US university, feature amenities such as a cafeteria serving free food, Internet lounges, a gymnasium, a pharmacy, and a hair salon—all of which contribute to a better quality of life.[3]

It also created new jobs in Chongqing, which helped open the door for other businesses and commerce to enter the region. The new facility helped us improve our operating margin and drive value back to our business.

At the same time, we helped establish a new freight train network from Chongqing to Germany, along the Trans-Eurasian Railway, to create easier access between central China and Europe. This alternative rail solution reduces CO_2e emissions by more than 90% compared with air freight and cuts costs by over 60%. The route is also 10 days faster than ocean transport.

Looking holistically at our supply chain in China, we were able to create an innovative solution that improves workers' lives, reduces environmental impact, and helps drive a more sustainable economy. This is Living Progress at work. And the journey doesn't end there. We continue to look for ways to

---

3 *New York Times* Video Report: http://www.nytimes.com/video/business/100000001974026/the-ieconomy-factory-upgrade.html

improve the lives of workers across our supply chain and raise the bar for the industry. In 2013, we introduced the 'HP Student and Dispatch Worker[4] Guidance Standard for Supplier Facilities in the People's Republic of China'. And in 2014, HP became the first company in the IT industry to require direct employment of foreign migrant workers in its supply chain, addressing the vulnerabilities that these workers face in outsourced employment relationships.

Engaging employees

Aligning strategy around a common purpose can also help engage and excite employees. In 2014, the HP Company Foundation[5] launched the 'Matter to a Million' employee engagement programme with Kiva, a non-profit organisation working to alleviate poverty by connecting people through micro lending. Through the Matter to a Million programme every HP employee received a US$25 credit to loan to a small business owner through Kiva. This five-year collaboration with Kiva gives HP employees multiple opportunities to contribute and be active participants in driving economic progress in global communities.

The response and enthusiasm has been staggering. In the first nine months, HP employees and the HP Company Foundation have supported more than US$5.8 million in microloans to entrepreneurs around the world, and some HP employees are choosing to drive additional impact by contributing their own funds directly to the Kiva programme.

Conclusion

It's easy to feel overwhelmed and discouraged by the tough social, economic and environmental challenges facing our world, but HP believes these challenges present opportunities for creativity and innovation. A new sustainable economy that advances human, economic, and environmental progress is not only possible, it's essential, and businesses must step up and drive this transformation.

Our journey to create a better future began with putting purpose at the heart of our strategy. As we continue to execute on our turnaround and prepare to separate into two Fortune 50 companies, having a clearly articulated vision of

---

4 Dispatch workers are temporary labourers provided by agencies.
5 Hewlett-Packard Company is the sole contributor to the Hewlett-Packard Company Foundation and has funded the Foundation throughout the last 35 years.

> **A new sustainable economy that advances human, economic and environmental progress is not only possible, it's essential, and businesses must step up and drive this transformation**

citizenship that's intertwined with our innovation, operations, and social investment provides us with an essential roadmap. We're realising this vision through innovations like Moonshot, Apollo, and The Machine that focus the creativity and talents of our employees on developing solutions that build a sustainable future for our business and for the global economy.

In her book, *A Better World, Inc.* (Korngold, 2014), Alice Korngold tells why global companies are uniquely suited to solve the world's problems and succeeding where governments and non-governmental organisations have not. Korngold argues that only global companies have the combination of 'human capital, technology, international scope, and incentives of the marketplace to build a better world', and she demonstrates through corporate case studies how companies are profiting by solving the world's toughest challenges.

At HP, we realise this possibility every day through the commitment, passion, and actions of our people united behind a common purpose to create a better future for everyone. We see this happening at other companies, like Unilever, Nike, and Interface, that put purpose at the heart of strategy, and as a result are transforming their industries and the world.

By adopting a purpose-driven strategy and integrating sustainability across their entire value chain, companies can capture return on capital today and build the leadership and business value for their future. These investments help companies create a competitive advantage, build stability, and provide assurances to stakeholders that they are well positioned for the challenges of the 21st century, all of which help accelerate a sustainable economy.

References

EY, (2014) 'Big data: Changing the way businesses compete and operate,' April 2014, page 24 (http://www.ey.com/Publication/vwLUAssets/EY_-_Big_data:_changing_the_way_businesses_operate/$FILE/EY-Insights-on-GRC-Big-data.pdf)

James, J., (2014) 'Data Never Sleeps 2.0,' April 23, 2014 (http://www.domo.com/blog/2014/04/data-never-sleeps-2-0/)

HP Labs (2014), 'HP Labs on the Data Explosion,' HP Matter: The Enterprise Issue, *Issue No. 1*, June 2014 (https://ssl.www8.hp.com/hpmatter/issue-no-1-june-2014/hp-labs-data-dilemma)

Global Footprint Network, 'World footprint: Do we fit on the planet,' http://www.footprintnetwork.org/en/index.php/GFN/page/world_footprint/

Korngold, A. (2014), *A Better World, Inc.*, Palgrave Macmillan®, New York, NY.

For Product Safety Concerns and Information please contact our EU
representative GPSR@taylorandfrancis.com Taylor & Francis Verlag GmbH,
Kaufingerstraße 24, 80331 München, Germany

Printed and bound by CPI Group (UK) Ltd, Croydon, CR0 4YY
01/05/2025
01858399-0005